Coffeehouse Resistance

Brewing Hope in Desperate Times

The Coffeehouse Resistance

Brewing Hope in Desperate Times

Sarina Prabasi

GREEN WRITERS PRESS | *Brattleboro, Vermont*

Printed in the United States

10 9 8 7 6 5 4 3 2 1

Green Writers Press is a Vermont-based publisher whose mission is to spread a message of hope and renewal through the words and images we publish. Throughout we will adhere to our commitment to preserving and protecting the natural resources of the earth. To that end, a percentage of our proceeds will be donated to environmental activist groups and for *The Coffeehouse Resistance*, a percentage from the sales of this book will go to Northern Manhattan Coalition for Immigrant Rights (NMCIR), a non-profit organization founded to educate, defend and protect the rights of immigrants. Green Writers Press gratefully acknowledges support from individual donors, friends, and readers to help support the environment and our publishing initiative.

GReen
wRITeRs
press

Giving Voice to Writers & Artists Who Will Make the World a Better Place
Green Writers Press | Brattleboro, Vermont • www.greenwriterspress.com

ISBN: 978-1-7328540-3-1

COVER DESIGN BY ASHA HOSSAIN DESIGN, LLC

INTERIOR ILUSTRATIONS BY CELINE SCHMIDT

THE PAPER USED IN THIS PUBLICATION IS PRODUCED BY MILLS COMMITTED
TO RESPONSIBLE AND SUSTAINABLE FORESTRY PRACTICES

To Elias, who makes everything possible.

CONTENTS

THE DOORS SLIDE OPEN and we walk through them, leaving JFK Airport with our large suitcases and our eighteen-month-old daughter. We are enveloped by the heat and the heavy humidity of New York City in July. That night we spend in a hotel near the airport. It has been a long journey and we all need some rest before we start the process of finding the apartment and turning it into our new home. Elias, Juni, and I are flight and hotel room veterans. In her short life, our daughter has already been on four continents. So that first night, we are comfortably ensconced in the calming (to us) space of a nondescript mid-range hotel chain, with its neutral colors and art on the walls that I'm sure were there, but that left no lasting impression. We sleep deeply.

When we get to the micro-neighborhood of Hudson Heights in Washington Heights, at the northern tip of Manhattan, it is at once familiar and new. Our taxi rolls up to an unfamiliar address and we are clumsy as we pay and struggle with our multiple bags and Juni in a baby carrier on my chest. We ring for the Super, who is holding keys to the apartment . . . which we have never seen. We searched for it and found it online on Craigslist while we were still in Ethiopia. My friend Sarah has gone to visit the apartment, and confirmed to us that the pictures in the ad were indeed of the apartment she saw.

As soon as we enter the apartment, I am crushed by a feeling, perhaps what claustrophobia might feel like. Even completely empty, it is so small. The rooms, kitchen, and bathroom are all shiny and clean, but I feel like a giant in a dollhouse. It is more oppressively humid than outside, if that is even possible. I feel a pang that might lead to panic, and wonder if we have made a colossal mistake. How could we, all three of us, possibly live here? I look directly at Elias for the first time since getting out of the taxi, and I see my own false-brave expression mirrored back on my husband's face. "It'll be fine. We'll be fine," I say, not sure if I'm trying to convince him or myself. I go to open the windows, but the humid stillness doesn't shift at all.

We have borrowed an air mattress, sheets, and a small table fan from my cousin. Juni senses our discomfort and is unusually fussy before falling asleep. At about nine at night, there is a knock on our door. The man at the door introduces himself as Ralph, our downstairs neighbor. He has heard that a couple with a baby has arrived from Africa and is now in the bare and empty apartment 5A. He has brought old towels and sheets to welcome us, he says, and hands them to me. Then he complains that he can hear the fan in our room and tells us we should know that the building is old, and sounds travel easily. I force the tight smile to stay on my face while we thank him. As soon as we close the door, I drop the pile of old towels and sheets. I wonder what we're going to do with these old towels, with a downstairs neighbor who can hear our fan, with an active daughter in a dollhouse apartment, in a city of millions with no job, no real connections. For the first time since we decided to move, I feel a little afraid.

Beginnings

THERE'S AN IRONY IN THE FACT that I am writing a memoir. Or perhaps it makes perfect sense. I have a deep fear of forgetting. I've had to let go of places, friends, family, over and over again. I've been on the move since childhood; staying is more noteworthy than leaving. In this swirl of places and people, I worry about losing moments held dearly. A loosening of my ability to bring back the precise, sharp, heart-pounding exhilaration of the moment or the dull throbbing of an ache. Blurring faces and images, confusing who said what, and who did what first. Forgetting is the opposite of the peace of voluntarily letting go. Instead, forgetting feels like my most precious possessions being stolen, silently, while I'm unaware. Moving so much means that I create and recreate home. Home is often a feeling rather than a place. I have a terrible memory for the things that I want to remember most.

My brother, on the other hand, remembers everything. He remembers what he couldn't possibly, because he was too young. He'll remember not only what we ate on that special night out as kids, but what the menu looked like and the conversation my parents had. He remembers the set of matchbox toy cars I gave him for his birthday, which I, five years older than him, don't remember.

I worry that I might have a memory disorder, though I've met other people who have porous memories like mine. Other times I've wondered whether this is a sign of something I've repressed, some trauma so deep that I am still running away from it, not wanting to acknowledge it. But my forgetting isn't limited to childhood. I worry that the busier I get, the more I do, the faster the forgetting fairy works. Memories of the recent past seem more distant than they should.

Taking photographs, writing, telling stories, these are all ways I fight the forgetting. In telling and retelling stories, I wonder how much of it is the actual memory, and how much of it is a now-practiced routine. Photographs are frustrating in their own way. They might serve as visual prompts, but they leave so much untold. They can't substitute memory, that is not their place. Of all my forgetfulness-fighting tools, writing is the best. In writing I can relive a memory or snatch back a detail I thought was lost forever and reclaim it as mine.

My mind is like a coarse sieve that lets too much fall through its mesh. The precious few grains, the memories that I rely on, and that stay with me, are of fleeting moments, of feelings, of smells. Small points of light as if that's where the flashlight had briefly pointed. The rest is darkness. And fear. Fear that when these bright spots leave me, I will be utterly alone in the darkness.

I'm surrounded by the excited chattering of children my own age. I recognize the intonations, the expressions, the gestures. I am comforted by them. I try not to think too much about where Mama has gone. I walk around touching things. I hold the brand new crayons to my face and inhale their familiar waxy scent. I look at the children closest to me, I examine their faces closely, wanting to recognize one of them, but I don't. I don't know anyone in the room. I can see their mouths moving, and I can hear the sounds coming out, but I can't understand a word of what they're saying.

As my anxiety starts to build, I approach Mrs. Sharma. *"Mero Mama kahile aunuhunchha?"* When is my Mama coming back? I ask her. She points to the clock, to the number twelve, and says, "Your mom will be here soon. Soon." It takes many years for me to realize that the English word soon doesn't in fact mean noon.

I think it is afternoon. We are in what I know now is a private hospital room. I wonder why the white-bright lights are on when the sun is streaming from the windows. There's a lot of white in the room: the sheets and the walls. It's not comfortable or cozy, but the kind of place where I feel I must be alert and stand straight. The smells in the room tickle my nose.

My dad has brought me to visit my mom and my new brother in the hospital. He is tiny, and bird-like, and pink. His eyes are covered with white bandages, and he is inside a transparent container, a machine, with bright bulbs shining on him. I want to climb into bed with Mama and snuggle under the covers with her. I don't think that I'm allowed to do this, so instead I edge up to the bed and try to get as close to her as I can. I can smell her perfume.

When the visitors come, I announce loudly that they can't hold my brother because they have germs and he is small and might get sick. I have now established a role for myself that will endure for decades. I am in charge. I am his protector. I still have an important role. I am not the only one, but I am the older one.

I love going to Julie's house, though it's always hard for me to recognize hers among so many similar houses neatly arranged in the gated compound. Julie's mom makes grilled cheese sandwiches for us, which I love. One day we're eating our favorite snack at her house when Julie tells me that she and her family are moving. They are going to the United States, because her father has a new job in a place called Michigan. My grilled cheese sandwich suddenly doesn't taste so good. I leave the rest of it uneaten on my plate. In fact, maybe something is wrong with it, I think, as my stomach starts to hurt.

We are on the bus, going home from school, on Julie's last day. We sit close, next to each other, and in my head, I count the number of stops left until hers. As the bus slows down and stops, she gives me a quick hug and kisses my cheek. Then she's gone. I promise myself right then that I will never wash my face again.

I'm in fifth grade when my mom tells me we're moving "back" to Nepal. Our childhood moves have made my brother and me co-conspirators in exploring new neighborhoods, shops, foods, and phrases. My mom is usually single-handedly in charge of the logistics, of packing and unpacking, creating and recreating a home for us wherever we may be.

We speak Nepali at home with our parents, but Samir and I cannot read or write our native language. Going to a Nepali school would mean going back several grades to compensate. Instead, our dad decides we will continue our international school education in Kathmandu. We are enrolled in the American international school, called Lincoln School, even though this is not the most financially prudent decision, even with a scholarship. Our father's life is one that has been transformed by education, catapulting him from a small and remote village in the Terai region of Nepal to teaching as an academic at an internationally acclaimed university, and later becoming a senior diplomat. He's not about to compromise on our education.

I am jubilant about our move. Our visits to Nepal are always full of family gatherings, delicious foods, and long afternoons spent with my many cousins. And life in Kathmandu for the first few months is like our regular visits, full of celebratory gatherings, traditional meals and lots of fuss over us kids. But after a few months in our new life in Kathmandu, we settle into a less exciting routine. My parents insist that Samir and I learn to read and write Nepali and arrange for a tutor to come to our home. While I want to learn, I find the lessons very boring and repetitive, and come up with all kinds of excuses to cut them short. Right before our tutor arrives, I decide to take a long shower. Or I urgently need to tell Mama something in the middle of the lesson. Too often I feign a stomachache or a headache, or an ache of any sort. I can read Nepali, but with great effort, and not very well.

No longer treated like VIP visiting guests, I begin to realize that for a girl who has just hit puberty, there are some big changes in my new life. There are rules for girls, and though my brother is years younger, I sense—though I can't immediately articulate it—that our roles in our family have shifted. He is the son. And I am not. I never feel this from my own parents, but my extended family's attitudes are much more traditional.

One such tradition is mortifying to me. I learn that when a woman has her period, it's not just her private business, but everyone's. This is because the woman is not allowed to cook, or eat with everyone else, or in some cases even enter certain rooms, like the kitchen, or in my case, my grandmother's room.

I've recently started my period, and with pressure from my grandmother (my father's mother is known for her ability to track of the number of days in each woman's cycle in her head), Mama sets my dinner up away from our dining table in a corner near the entrance to our kitchen. When my dad came to the table, he asks where I am. When he learns that I will not be sitting at the table for our evening meal, he is furious. His voice is raised and sharp. "I am not educating my daughter so that she can be treated as a lesser human being. Sarina will eat with us, at this table, every day of the month. End of story."

I eat dinner that evening with my family and understand that my dad will stick up for me, and that his voice is heard in a way that Mama's isn't. This is just one of the times he's cleared the way for me so that I can blaze my own path.

I imagine that we meet again after all these years.

"I still remember those cranes, Keiko," I offer tentatively.

"Do you?" She smiles.

"How did you fold a thousand origami cranes during our exams? Your parents must have been so mad." I am smiling too, with equal parts long-held curiosity and admiration.

"Yeah, my mom wasn't happy when she found out. I hid them, but when they started piling up, they were harder to hide."

"I've wondered what you thought about while you were folding them. I've wondered how come you didn't just give up after a hundred."

"I didn't have anything to give you for your birthday. Remember how strict my parents were? It was a minor miracle that I was even allowed to sleep over at your house." After a pause, she adds, "I haven't thought about those cranes for a long time."

---

[1] *Senbazuru*, or a group of one thousand origami paper cranes held together by strings. An ancient Japanese legend promises you will be granted a wish by the gods.

After school we head to Hem's in Thamel, a bustling area of gift shops, bars, and restaurants. We pass shops selling pashmina scarves, silver and turquoise jewelry, bronze statues, embroidered T-shirts and hand-printed bedcovers. It's an area still popular with tourists. We are not tourists, we are cool locals, and we are not here to shop. Exams are coming, and it's crunch time. We need to do some serious studying.

Petra and I are close and often need few words to communicate. With a tilt of the head, a glance, and a simple "Hem's?" we decide to go. We climb the circular stairs, going up to the roof terrace of a familiar place that is not home, not school, but a place that is our own, nonetheless. In my bag is the latest mix-tape cassette that will provide the perfect soundtrack for our studies. "Hey, dai, how are you?" we greet the manager who is also the waiter and bartender. I hand him my laboriously created mix-tape and he needs no further explanation.

The place is deserted. Perfect. Soon Tracy Chapman's voice and acoustic guitar surround us. We take the best table, a four-top under a sun umbrella so we're outside but in the shade and we can spread out our notebooks, books, and highlighters. Our drinks, bubbly soda sweetened with simple syrup and flavored with freshly squeezed lime juice soon appear on our table—sweet lime sodas are a favorite. We sit diagonally from each other so we can prop up our feet on the opposite chair—no dangling legs for studying in true comfort. Content now, we concentrate.

Ray's jeans are so soft. Their indigo has faded into a light blue memory. They fit well, but not too snugly around my waist. When I walk they shift slightly, reminding me that they are my boyfriend's borrowed jeans. I think of them every time I read "boyfriend jeans," now a style of jeans described in a catalog.

One afternoon I trip and fall and they rip just above my right knee. After I wash and clean up my bleeding knee, I patch the tear with a vibrant red and black patterned fabric. There is now no question of my giving these jeans back to Ray. I stop thinking of them as borrowed; they are truly mine.

As can be the way with these things, as deeply as I love these jeans, my mom hates them. Or perhaps she hates the implications. That I am walking around wearing a boy's jeans. A boy that I don't hide. A boy so handsome and polite, a boy from a different ethnic group and caste than ours. These differences are alive and well in Nepal. Ray's family are Newars—the original inhabitants of the old Kathmandu valley. My family is Brahmin, and though my parents are not "strict," the unspoken rule between our two groups is that friendships and socializing are fine; relationships and marriage are forbidden.

For me these jeans are as much about me as they are about him. Yes, there is the thrilling intimacy of wearing a man's jeans. No, not just men's jeans, but his. My motorcycle-riding, leather-jacket-wearing, dark-haired, stubble-cheeked and dimple-chinned boyfriend's jeans. Equally thrilling to me is my own boundary-breaking, not-hiding, not-lying, out-in-the-open relationship-displaying. I am taking my first steps of independence, and they are sometimes as shaky as my first actual baby steps might have been. But these jeans are an emblem to me of the choices I can make. That I can defy the judgment of the culture in which I grew up. And get away with it. I don't remember asking Ray for his jeans. I don't know how I got them. But I love them. They are one of my prized possessions.

I will soon be leaving home to go to college. After high school graduation, I will fly to New York City where I'll spend the summer with my cousin, my one relative in the United States, before going on to a small town in Massachusetts. A private liberal arts college has offered me a generous scholarship.

Everything I want to take with me has to fit into two suitcases. One of the first things I pack are the jeans that are now undeniably mine. After the tears and goodbyes at the airport, after I tell my mom that I probably wouldn't be back for a long time (oh, the self-absorbed cruelty of adolescence!), after the flight and the connecting flight and the wide-awake hours of overexcitement on a dark plane, after arriving movie-like into a city with yellow cabs and bright lights, the following day when I finally unpack my suitcases in my cousin's apartment I can't find those jeans anywhere. I go through every single piece of clothing before the sinking realization that my mom has taken them out, those jeans she hates so much. At first I am furious, but then I feel a grudging respect, and within a few moments, I start to laugh.

The phone line crackles and I realize that it's very early in the morning for my mom. Yikes, I haven't checked the time difference. In the pot, bay leaves and whole peppercorns are sizzling in oil, and on the chopping board are finely diced onions and ginger, tomatoes, and cilantro. But I'm stuck, because I know I'm forgetting something. It's my first time cooking my mom's special fish curry alone.

In the dead of winter, in western Massachusetts, frigid air comes in from the window I've propped open in a futile attempt to prevent the whole house from absorbing the pungent fragrance of fish curry. It's important that this curry comes out just right, though the main ingredient, the fish, is improvised. I can't find rahu machha here, so I picked a white fish that I have fried and very gently put aside so it doesn't fall apart in the curry.

I've called my mom to ask her what I'm forgetting. Of course, it's the mustard seeds. I have them in the spices I've brought from home, a circle of little round bowls nestled inside a circular stainless steel container. These spice kits are in every home in Nepal, and my mom carefully packed one for me when I was leaving home.

"The mustard makes all the difference. The red kind. Rayo, make sure you use rayo," my mom explains. I think it's all just called mustard in English, but in Nepali there are at least three different kinds, each with its own name.

Though I'm fluent in English and my new college friends in Massachusetts often comment that I have no accent (they mean I don't have a "foreign" accent), I am most comfortable with the Nepali names of spices and ingredients while I'm cooking. I say their names out loud as I chop, dice, and slice, and it makes me ache for home.

I've always lived in the hustle and bustle of capital cities—New Delhi, Beijing, Kathmandu—and I'm convinced that nothing will live up to what I have left behind. I'm having more difficulty adjusting this first year than I care to admit, even to myself. It's not that I don't make friends, but that I miss my old friends deeply.

Looking back, I'm struck by how old-fashioned it feels to remember the ridiculously expensive international phone calls, my parents' voices sounding strange and distant over the crackling connection. And me, hanging up the phone, unsatisfied and somehow feeling worse and more alone than ever. I don't outwardly display my deep melancholy. Though I am worldly and well-traveled, this is this is my first time away from my family. I sleep too much, I eat too much, and most days I walk around with a lead weight in the pit of my stomach. I don't have words for what I am experiencing, and I don't know who or how to ask for help.

I find it difficult to study in my room during the day. I miss my Kathmandu café study sessions with Petra. Sometimes I go to the library, where I also work. I work many different jobs on campus with the work-study portion of my scholarship package. Working at the library is my favorite, followed closely by score-keeping for the field hockey team, a job I've been recruited into by my hockey-playing roommate. Doing dishes in the cafeteria kitchen is my least favorite, and I am overwhelmed by the mounds of food that gets wasted, thrown away every day. Stuffing envelopes in the Admissions Office, answering questions in the Career Development Office, waitressing at the Faculty Club, and cleaning rooms and getting the buildings ready for the summer Alumnae reunions are other jobs I do over the years.

One day I'm walking down Main Street and I see a small sign—Haymarket Café. When I step into the space, I am enveloped by it. The place is rundown in a comfortable way, with mismatched second-hand soft chairs and armchairs, scratched tables, a soft and warm glow emanating from lamps spread out across the space and not a fluorescent light in sight. The coffee smells wonderful, but the most spectacular, wonderful thing of all: stacks of used books are everywhere. Some are tatter-covered, others are good-quality hard covers—there are books of all types in all conditions just waiting to be browsed through. Amidst all of this is a counter serving coffee and tea, drinks, pastries, and sandwiches. I feel a child-like delight bubble up inside me. I probably stand there and grin for a long while.

On one wall is a small but prominently placed sign. It explains that the café is named in honor of the "Haymarket Affair" in Chicago where, on May 4, 1886, working men and women took to the streets on behalf of workers' rights, including the eight-hour work day. The rally at Haymarket Square started out as a peaceful protest and ended in deaths, injuries, and violence. It led to the commemoration of International Workers Day, or "May Day," around the world.

There are a mix of people at the café. Some are students from Smith, but others look like townies of various age groups. Two gray-haired men with ponytails are engrossed in a game of chess. I browse through the books, I order a latte, and observe the place and the people. I try not stare at others but watch them discreetly. I'm interested in learning about what goes on at Haymarket Café.

The next day, I return prepared with my backpack filled with coursework from my economics, post-colonial literature, and anthropology classes. I come with friends from my dorm sometimes, but what I remember most is sitting in an old chair, with a slightly too-low table in front of me, drinking a latte and studying. The hum and hiss of the espresso machines in the background, the music (never too loud), the sounds of plates and glasses clanking, people chatting, laughing, meld into a punctuated hum that is the perfect background for me to focus and concentrate.

These are my latte-with-two-spoonfuls-of-sugar days. If I stay beyond three hours, then I will order a second one. As I knew the moment I first stepped into the space, the Haymarket Café and I become close, regular companions for the rest of my time in Northampton. It is a place I can spend hours, losing myself in the eclectic selection of books, if I let myself, or when I am being more disciplined, concentrating on my assignment at hand. Outside my dorm room and the library, Haymarket Café is where I do most of my reading, writing, and thinking.

I breathe in deeply and struggle with buttoning my jeans and zipping them up. *Must be the dryer,* I think to myself, though I know it's no such thing. I am lost here in the whiteness of the snow, this picture-postcard-perfect scene from the window, but there is only numbness inside. I sprinkle *dhulo achaar* from Nepal and made by my aunt. I ration it, sprinkling a little on the thick creamy soups, or the salads, or the rubber chicken breasts. The food in the dining hall is bland but plentiful and I am eating more than I ever have before. I've mastered my fake smile and excel at superficial conversations. Inside I am counting the minutes until I can be home again. This is more than homesickness, but it will be years before I can name what ails me.

At nineteen, my friend Melissa and I admit our deep desire to escape the unfathomable (to us) Massachusetts winter. On a lazy, dark, and depressing afternoon approaching winter break, we point to the world map on my wall and narrow down our choices based on budget and where we might wrangle some free accommodation. We are resourceful, reaching out to the friends and friends-of-friends not only at Smith but throughout the interconnected five college system. We make this trip happen, we will it into being, and we make it to Jamaica on the cheapest of flights and two hundred dollars in our pockets.

In an old and rusty pickup truck, over deeply cratered roads, we leap and bounce at considerable speed. Despite being jostled around like a sack of potatoes, I am in heaven in the back of this truck. I look out to the blue and gold of the shore, which is increasingly distant as we circle up the mountains. Soon the ocean and the glittering sands are just a memory. As the air cools and we drive through forests, I imagine the oxygen the trees are exuding and breathe easier.

I'm headed to the Blue Mountains of Jamaica, where the world-famous Blue Mountain Coffee comes from. At the time, I have no interest in coffee. That all comes later.

`

Addis Ababa

SMILE FROM EAR TO EAR as I stride down 19th Street. I can't contain my energy and excitement, and I don't care that I'm smiling at strangers. Liz, one of my bosses at the nonprofit agency where I am an assistant to everyone, has just told me that she would like me to accompany her to help an evaluation of our program in Ethiopia. I'm delighted at the opportunity and the compliment within it—the trip feels like something I have earned. A further bonus, not to be dismissed: I will escape a chunk of Washington, DC in January.

I've heard my dad tell stories of Addis Ababa from his travels in the late 1960s during Emperor Haile Selassie's reign. He's told me of a beautiful city with purple Jacaranda-lined boulevards. Now, years later, I arrive late at night to a dimly lit airport. I'm supposed to look for the hotel shuttle, and as I make my way outside, I pass soldiers standing in twos, looking serious with long rifles hanging over their shoulders. I've never seen so many guns.

Once I get outside the airport, the air is chilly. I can feel the difference in altitude in my lungs, coming from swampy Washington, DC. I can't see them yet in the dark, but I can sense the mountains around me. I'm a stranger here, but my body relaxes and I feel oddly at home. I'm smiling widely by the time I find my hotel shuttle driver.

At breakfast the next morning, Liz and I finish reviewing our meetings for the day. "And then, we must go to Tomoca." she says as a matter of decided fact. Liz and her husband lived in Addis in the 1970s and were married in the city; it holds a special place in her heart and life story. On this trip, she takes me under her wing and allows me to tag along as she retraces her footsteps to her old haunts. In fact, bringing me to Ethiopia on this work assignment was her idea. I am lucky that my initial introduction to the country is by someone who has a deep fondness for it. It colors my own first impressions.

I sense Tomoca is a special place as soon as we enter. The smell of roasted coffee permeates not only the air, but the walls, the furniture, the people—all seem coffee-infused. I know when we leave this coffee smell will linger in my hair, and on my clothes and skin.

The one-room establishment is high-ceilinged, and fans spin lazily over our heads. Late-afternoon sun streams through the dusty windows. There is no place to sit, only tall tables that people, mostly men, lean over as they slurp coffee served in small glasses. A few are reading newspapers, and others are chatting animatedly. I imagine they are talking about politics or sports, though I can't understand a word. I am curious to explore the maps and the photos on the wall.

We pay first and get tokens in return. You take the tokens to the back and the color of your token tells the guy what type of coffee you want. "And Sarina, you have to buy coffee—if you want to take some home with you—you have to buy it here." Again, Liz says this as a fact. Clearly I shouldn't consider buying coffee anywhere else.

Liz cheerfully chats in Amharic with the woman behind the cash register. After we pay, she tells me that she and her husband, Terry, had lived in a small apartment very close to Tomoca, and had been frequent customers.

I notice a display of different shades of roasted coffee in clear dispensers along one wall. The first dispenser contains beans that are very dark—they are almost black and slightly burnt looking. In the dispenser next to it are beans, still dark, but a slightly softer brown, shiny and oily. Finally there are lighter brown beans that look dry. I take my token to the counter along the back wall and silently pass it with a smile to the older gentleman behind the counter wearing a uniform, a white jacket that looks like a lab coat. The uniform and his expression display a gravitas—making coffee is serious business, I guess. He nods, acknowledging the token I give him, and the espresso machine behind him started to hiss.

When he hands me my drink, it is served in a clear glass with a white saucer and a slightly wet demitasse spoon nestled on the saucer. My macchiato is beautiful. The glass perfectly displays the layers of white and brown, steamed milk and espresso, with a little bit of foam on top. I thank the gentleman, take my drink, and head over to the standing tables. They have filled up since our arrival, and so Liz and I share one with a group of three men who seem to be friends and regular customers—they call out greetings to the staff and to other people as they come in. Their coffees are served in a similar glass, but they are drinking theirs black. I can see granules of sugar—an opaque melting layer settled at the bottom of their glasses.

I pick up my own glass, blow on it a little, and take my first sip. A rich, deep flavor, sweet and the perfect balance of strong coffee and steamed milk, greets my taste buds. Halfway through my drink, I say to Liz, "I think I want another one."

That first two-macchiato visit to Tomoca begins my long love affair with the drink. Every day while I am in Addis, I seek out places to drink macchiato. The worst macchiato I drink is served at the expensive hotel where we are staying. The best, in small streetside cafes and *bunna-betoch*: coffeehouses.

I now visit Ethiopia regularly for work, a couple of times a year. Five years have passed since that first trip, and I've gotten to know and love the country— it's vast expanses, its diversity of landscape and languages. I've traveled to some of the most neglected and distant parts of the lush South, and rocky North. I love the foods, avidly follow the latest Ethiopian pop music, and I'm conversant in the basics of Amharic.

I'm having an administrative problem, which might be easily solved, except that I have a Nepali passport and a US green card. The fact that I am applying for a UK visa at the British Embassy in Addis Ababa has apparently broken all bureaucratic protocols and I need to go and sort this out in person at the visa section at the Embassy, where I will no doubt have to spend most the day, or perhaps even the next few days. It's a huge distraction, and I'm annoyed, as I always am, when I'm confronted with barriers that I fundamentally disagree with.

Outside my office, I'm looking for a taxi. In these days, they're tiny, Russian-made Ladas painted white on top and blue around the body of the car. I see one, open the door to get in, and there is the driver, sprawled out, seat reclined, knees up and almost touching the steering wheel. He barely fits in the tiny car. Before I even tell him where I'm going, I tease him about his two-passenger car, since there clearly isn't room for anyone in the seat behind him. I'm hyper-aware, all my senses heightened and on alert. *Pay attention, this is important*, my whole being seems to instruct me. All I remember about that first taxi ride is him.

A year later, I move to Addis Ababa and I see the taxi guy again. This time we are introduced by his childhood friend, who works in my office. His name is Elias, and he grew up and still lives in the neighborhood where I work. I run into him occasionally. I don't remember who asked who, but we end up at a coffee shop called Peacock. We park in front and a waiter comes to the car. Elias orders our macchiatos. *"Endworede, eishi?"* Always eager to improve my Amharic vocabulary, I ask him what *"endworede"* means. I say the word slowly, *en-dwo-re-de*, going over each syllable and rolling the "r." Elias smiles at my slow enunciation.

Then he frowns, thinking. "Hmm . . . how do I explain this in English? It means fresh. Straight from the machine. Like freshly-squeezed juice," Elias says. I love the sounds of the word, and as I repeat the syllables with him, I notice the timbre of his voice, the fluidity in his long limbs. There is something oddly intimate about sitting in a car and drinking coffee with a man. We are cocooned in a private space of our own, in a vehicle that isn't going anywhere, drinking the most heavenly of drinks.

It becomes our custom to meet for macchiato. And our favorite place is Peacock on Bole Road. The place is gone now, but my memories of macchiatos there, perfectly steamed and layered, so satisfying, are vivid still. And the waiters at Peacock are an institution. Though they wear uniforms, identical mustard colored jackets, their personalities are distinct: the gravitas of the quiet and focused one, the chatty, friendly, popular one, the youngest of the group is taken away during one of the police crackdowns in Addis and returns shaved-headed and subdued. Their names have long-faded from my memory, but not the taste of the macchiatos they served.

But in those early days, having a macchiato is a reason to meet, a reason to spend an hour, then two and more together. When we are together time accelerates, and our goodbyes always come too soon. We rank the macchiatos we drink and plan trips to explore the seemingly endless number of places in Addis Ababa where one can get a great macchiato.

"Sarina, there's this place, but it's really small, there are some chairs and tables in the back, like a backyard. The macchiato is so very good, but I'm not sure if you'll be comfortable there." He pauses, and wrinkles his nose, making a face. "And you absolutely can't use the bathroom there. It's terrible."

"Okay, I don't need to use the bathroom. Let's go. Elias, let's go now, I'd love to try it."

The place is called Ruth. When Elias says it, it sounds like the word "root." The only spots of green in the backyard are a few potted plants and the branches of a brittle-looking tree that leans over from the other side of the wall dividing the property from the neighbor's. The rough, unfinished concrete floor has a couple of white plastic tables and chairs that have absorbed dust and grime that won't come off, no matter how vigorously the waitstaff wipes. The front of the house is a small bakery. I can still smell the freshly baked bread and feel the texture of the large, round rolls, crispy and crackly on the outside and as soft as clouds on the inside. The macchiato is amazing, creamy and strong and perfectly balanced. That bread and a shared order of *enkulal firfir*, Ethiopian-style scrambled eggs with onions, tomatoes, and green chilies, along with a couple of macchiatos, becomes a favorite breakfast of ours.

The waiter there, an adolescent boy from the northern part of Ethiopia, is always delighted to see us because he knows he will get a good tip. I often giggle when I call him over to our table for another round of macchiatos because his name, Yene Sow, literally translates to "my man." I feel a little shy every time I call to him.

Over many forays like this, I learn the nuances of ordering a perfect macchiato. I can say *tukur macchiato* if I want it dark and strong, I can say *netalaya* if I want a medium and well-balanced version, and I can say *nech* if I want the drink to come out beige and milky. And of course, *endworede*, that word so tricky to translate, some combination of made to order and fresh-squeezed. A good philosophy for living life itself.

It is just before the national elections in Ethiopia, and and the government is displaying an openness that is unexpected. Ethiopia will have its first televised political debates, and I am struck by the energy around politics and discussions of the upcoming elections. Old ladies and young children smile and flash the "V" sign with their hands, implying their support for the new opposition unity party, called Kenejit. The nascent party has limited resources and is going against a well-oiled established ruling party. But seemingly out of nowhere, towards the end of the campaign, Kenejit is making huge gains.

The night before the election, I have a party at my house. My mom is visiting and makes her special Nepali chicken. We have a lovely gathering of people, including some guests who leave early because they are volunteering at the polls in the morning.

The next day, the rumors start. Something has gone wrong. There are reports of arrests. Still, we all hold on to our optimism. For a historic election like this, some ups and downs are to be expected. It is reported that 90% of registered voters have gone to the polls. I hear that one of the guests at my party, a human rights lawyer who had planned to be monitoring the polling sites, has also been arrested.

The ruling party, the Ethiopian Peoples' Revolutionary Democratic Front, or EPRDF, has suffered an embarrassing defeat in Addis Ababa, and in many other parts of the country. The extent of support the Kenejit party was able to garner has stretched the EPRDF's tolerance, and like a rubber band, it has snapped back. Elias comes over the next day to tell me about the bad news that is trickling out. A state of emergency is declared.

"My friend's missing. Some people from the

neighborhood said he was arrested. I promised his mom I'd look for him."

"I'll go with you."

"I don't know how long it will take."

"It doesn't matter."

On our drive, the city streets are deserted. We pass a car that is in flames, but there is no one around for us to ask what's happened. We drive to the local jail. We are able to verify that Elias's friend is in the prison. Elias is not able to meet with him, but he is able to get information to the family and agree on the logistics of bringing in food and other supplies.

Later that afternoon, I receive a phone call from a friend, who also happens to be high up in the political party.

"Hello, Sarina, I'm calling to make sure you are okay."

"I'm okay, but a lot of people are not."

"Are you scared?"

"Should I be? No, I'm not scared. But I am scared for my Ethiopian friends and colleagues. What is going on? How can this be happening?"

"Don't worry. Things will settle down. I'll make sure you are safe. And the other things, these distur-bances, they will settle down over time. If you need anything, call me."

I hang up the phone, deeply disturbed. I am fine. As a foreigner, I have never felt unsafe in Ethiopia. But what I heard on the phone doesn't reassure me at all about my Ethiopian friends.

One night Elias and I are together at my house. We have lost track of time and it has gotten very late. He will be walking back to his home, but under the current political circumstances and the tension in the city, I urge him to leave before it gets any later.

The next morning, he doesn't come to pick me up as we have arranged. I try his phone, but it is switched off. I think perhaps he has forgotten to charge his phone, or he has overslept. But in the pit of my stomach, there is a feeling of dread and a disquiet that I can't shake off. I go to the office in a taxi and try to focus on my work. But every half an hour or so, I call his number and get no response.

Finally, in the early afternoon, I am able to reach him. I am so relieved to hear his voice, but also suddenly angry. "Elias, this is really not fair, I was worried about you."

"I'm okay. I'll explain when I see you. What time will you be finished with work?" His tone is sober, and I know, as my gut has told me all along, that he hasn't overslept.

When my workday is finally over, I rush outside. He is parked just outside my office. I get into the passenger seat and look at him.

"What happened?"

"They took me. The police."

"What? Are you okay? Did they hurt you?" I am aware of my voice rising and take some deep breaths to steady myself.

"I kept telling them, I'm just going home. I'm not causing any trouble. But they said there had been a disturbance in the area and they were looking for suspects. They picked up a whole bunch of us. Anyone who was walking outside at that time."

I watch his face. For once I have no words. I nod for him to continue.

"They took us all to the police station and kept us outside in the compound all night. They confiscated our phones, said they were going to check who we had been talking to."

"Are you okay? Did they hurt you?" I realize as I'm speaking that I am repeating myself. I hold both of his hands in mine. My eyes scan his whole body, from the top of his head to his feet.

"Yeah, I'm okay. Just mad." And then he smiles.

"Okay, let's go home."

After that day, if Elias is over at my place and it gets late, I insist that he stay over. I get no argument from him.

Soon after this incident, one afternoon I step out to the coffee shop next to my office to meet Elias. He is waiting for me when I get there, and we both order our usual macchiatos. An Ethiopian pop song that I like is playing in the background, and I sing along. Elias and I are making plans for the coming weekend. In a lull in our conversation, I notice that the café is suddenly quiet. I look up and around and notice two men wearing leather jackets and sunglasses, reading their newspapers. They look to be in their late twenties or early thirties. I have never seen them here before. I look at Elias and see him looking over at them, too.

He asks for our check, we pay and walk out. I start to say something, and he quickly shakes his head. "We'll talk later. I'll pick you up at 5:30, okay?"

That afternoon, my thoughts keep returning to the two men. The whole vibe in the café changed after they arrived. And they were not being inconspicuous, either. They clearly were not regulars in the local, off-the-main-road, small café, where everyone knows each other.

I am starting to see a side of Ethiopia I have not seen before. Elias tells me that a guy has been following him. "He keeps turning up wherever I go." He came to the *kebele*, the local club where Elias often meets his friends for beers and a game of *kerombola* (a table-top game played in many bars in Ethiopia). I don't know what to make of this, but I am increasingly worried about Elias.

So many young men have been picked up and taken out of the city to prisons and camps. At one of our regular haunts, I ask our waiter about his colleague, another waiter we haven't seen for a few days. His friendly and gregarious nature makes his absence keenly noticed. Our waiter sadly shakes his head.

"They took him. They took him too."

This could mean anything. He might be back soon. He might not. It's so difficult to get news of those who have been picked up and taken away. I worry if Elias is late; I worry about him when he is not with me. Finally, I decide to call my friend, the one high up in the political party.

"Hello, Sarina."

"Hi. How are you?"

"I'm well. Is everything okay?"

"I'm calling with a request."

"Of course, what is it? What do you need?"

"I'm calling for a friend. He was randomly picked up and held overnight in a prison. And now he's being followed, and harassed. I want it to stop." My voice sounds angry even to my own ears, though I am trying my best to the feelings from my voice. I want this to be a simple logistical request, not something that will raise more alarm bells.

"Eishi. I understand. Let me find out and I'll call you back."

The next day he calls. "It won't be a problem anymore. You don't need to worry."

"Thank you."

"It's okay. Take care."

This is surreal. I hope I can believe him.

Over the next few days I keep asking Elias if he notices the guy following him.

"No, that guy just disappeared. Maybe he got bored."

"Good. Stay boring." I smile.

The shade is cool under the bottlebrush trees in our garden. The temperatures fall perfectly at night to a chill, inviting me to pull the covers closer around us in bed. I think about our rooster and hens, and the entertaining hours spent watching their antics as they peck at the grass and dirt and squawk and chase each other and basically spend all their waking hours eating. But the mushroom stems, that's what they fight each other for. It is my pleasure after slicing up some mushrooms for an omelet or stir-fry to go outside with the stems that I have trimmed and toss them near the chicken coop. The only other thing that gets them into that tizzy of excitement—of snatching pieces out from each other's mouths—is lettuce, particularly the inner succulent crispy parts of a head of lettuce.

Nothing goes to waste. Between the dogs, the chickens, and the compost, all organic materials are consumed and recycled by nature and returned to the earth. And while there is no formal recycling of paper and plastics, there is plenty of creative reuse. Plastic bottles are collected and reused, plastic bags are reused, and increasingly we are seeing reusable shopping bags made of the plastic bags that milk is sold in, and flip flops made from old plastic bags. People are so resourceful. Necessity is the mother of invention. I'll never forget seeing Kume, our housekeeper, wash and reuse disposable diapers for her baby son, Imran. Who knew that you could do that with Pampers? I later buy her reusable diapers, but she is doing quite well getting several weeks use out of one regular "disposable" diaper.

We have fresh eggs that are sometimes mysteriously hidden away in the bushes but are treasured nonetheless. Our eggs taste completely different from what we are used to buying at our local supermarket. Their yolks are a lustrous, vibrant orange. I enlist the help of a local carpenter, and commission a hen house thanks to some designs and photographs I find online to house them in what Elias calls their "designer house."

I think about the parties. The dinners, the dancing, and the music. I've grown to love Ethiopian traditional and pop music and eskista dancing. I am proud of the flexibility and the rhythm I've developed in my shoulders, and I deeply enjoy what most foreigners simply call "shoulder dancing." We host small, intimate dinners, casual lunches in the garden, and parties with booze and a live band and an elaborate buffet. Other times we stay in, cocooned blissfully in our deepening relationship and dig the soil and nurture it. We rearrange the furniture on a regular basis, we blast our favorite music from an old-fashioned speaker system, we cook for each other, we love.

In addition to our flower garden, we have a vegetable garden that I spend many hours planning and plotting out on paper. Elias and Aweke, who helps around the house and garden, dig the soil and add many bags of manure. The first bounty is the salad. We have a multitude of lettuces and salad greens in all hues of green, red, and purple. Next come the considerable quantities of radish, zucchini, and tomatoes. A major highlight of my weekends is checking on the vegetables, picking what is ready. Most of all I love the just-before-dinner salad picking. As a natural next step from gardening, we discover composting and delight in it. We have the unconditional love of three dogs, Addis Ababa mix I call them, whenever anyone asks about their breed. They are all rescues of one form or another, and they enrich our lives with their antics.

It is a happy home. Do we argue? Of course. But I remember it as a happy time of growing love.

Elias and I are content living together. We are committed to each other, we are in love, and that is enough. We agree that we don't need the state or a religious official to validate our relationship. We are just fine building our life together. Many of our Ethiopian friends and his family treat us like a married couple anyway.

But when we start thinking about wanting to have a child, that changes, and we decide to get married. Elias's proposal to me is more pragmatic than romantic, but it is one of deep love. If we want to have a child together—by any means, whether it's a child of our blood and bones or one of our heart through adoption—we are old-fashioned enough to think we should get married. Then there are the logistics. Elias is an Ethiopian citizen. I'm a Nepali citizen with a US green card. Without the proper paperwork, we're not sure of the implications for any future kids of ours.

So begin the preparations for the only Ethiopian-Nepali wedding that we know of. From the outset, Elias has set down some rules with Fifi, his mom. (Fifi raised him, and he never calls her his stepmother.) No parading around the city posing in the early morning light, no hotels nor large rental halls; a small wedding, a tiny one, a personal and private one, he insists. Fifi is a practical woman, and an untraditional one in so many ways. But when I say no bridesmaids, she is crestfallen and looks at me for a long time, "But what is it? Is it the expense?"

"No Fifi, we just want a simple wedding. We want the wedding to match us, to match our personalities."

"Well, if that's what you want." She sighs.

We win some battles and lose others. Fifi wins all the food battles and we have a veritable feast, prepared over many days under Fifi's guidance and supervision and with help from many of her friends and relatives. They gather in the kitchen and sing wedding songs while they chop, pound, clean, and wash the collard greens, shallots, onions, garlic, ginger, tomatoes, and many other ingredients that will go into our Ethiopian wedding feast.

"Hey, I hired you because we've known each other for a long time. But don't be telling me turn this way, turn that way, or do this or that. Because then you'll be fired. Just catch the natural moments." I smile with love for my husband-to-be as he speaks with the wedding photographer.

Leading up to our wedding day we spend time with visiting relatives and introduce the Nepali side of the family to the Ethiopian side of the family over meals, and yes, drinks and dancing. Coffee ceremonies. Evening outings to our favorite places in Addis and meals at our favorite restaurants. At an Armenian restaurant called Aladdin, one of our absolute favorites, the waitress comes and takes my eight-month-old nephew from my cousin's arms and says, "You eat, I'll play with the baby." She says it genuinely. My cousins visiting from New Jersey look visibly relieved, and they eat and take part in grown-up dinner conversation. Anyone who has small children can attest that simply eating uninterrupted can seem like a small miracle when your child is near. We enjoy our delicious dinner of flat bread and kebabs, *manti*, and my absolute favorite, *imam beyeldi*, which translates to "the imam fainted." That's how good it is, you could faint, especially if someone else is holding your child.

We are married under the bottlebrush trees in our garden, in a ceremony that is unique, surrounded by people who love us. We are married by an Ethiopian Orthodox priest and also have a simplified Hindu ceremony.

That night, for the reception, our compound is transformed into a magical venue. On the round, white-covered tables are candles and flowers, and an Ethiopian feast of so many colors. Fiery berbere-infused red sauce and milder yellow onion-based sauces flavor the meats, the softest collards chopped more finely by hand than one can imagine, home-made cheese, large round home-baked *dabo*, and of course rolls of *enjera*. The food looks gorgeous and is laid out on a long white cloth-covered table. The polite arguments about whether or not beef would be served have been long-forgotten.

Soon the music is pulsing, and the dancing begins. As the whiskey and *arake* and *tejj* flow, the dancing gets wilder. A group of friends hoist Elias on their shoulders, and a minute later, another group of friends surrounds me, and with remarkable strength and more gracefully than I could have imagined, lifts me up too. They bounce us both to the beat of the music.

The Nepali contingent makes up in enthusiasm what they lack in numbers. They play traditional Nepali folk songs, and as the music changes, so does the dancing, shifting from shoulders to undulating waists, arms and expressive hands. Many more people come than we invite. Thoughtfully they come after dinner, and bring alcohol with them, smiling as they arrive, "Hey, we heard Elias was getting married. How could we not be here?" Rather than being annoyed, I am deeply touched by this sign of how loved Elias is, here on his home turf.

It's Sunday morning, and we are snuggled in bed. I know what I have to do, and my heart is racing as I try to deepen my shallow breaths. I stocked up on home pregnancy tests during our last trip to London. Now I'm going to use the first one.

I bring the thermometer-like white plastic stick back with me from the bathroom and place it on our nightstand. I get back into bed and hold Elias and scrunch my eyes closed while I count the seconds in my head. I tell myself that it doesn't matter. But it does. In fact, my deepest wish at this moment is the outcome that I have happily and determinedly avoided for so many years. I feel the warmth of his skin next to mine, our breaths matching each inhale and exhale. I wait longer than the instructions indicate. Then, when waiting became impossible, I sit up in bed.

With eyes still closed, I reach for the plastic test stick. Slowly, I open my eyes to an aqua-blue plus sign.

My heart leaps, and yet my voice is a whisper.

"Elias, look."

We are smiling from ear to ear.

"Oh my god," Elias says.

We hold each other, our smiles getting in the way of our kisses.

After a while, I say, "I want to call my parents. It's too early to tell anyone, but I want to tell them."

I take out my tiny chocolate-brown flip phone and call my parents. My dad's voice is husky, "Sarina, I didn't know if I would see this day, but I am so, so, happy."

During the early days of pregnancy, my body, so familiar to me, takes on a newness, and I pay close attention to each sign, each change in my physical self. When I feel the baby's first movements, I am sitting with my feet up on an orange Ikea reclining chair in our living room. I feel a quickening in my belly. And then, as if a fish is jumping in water. I laugh out loud in delight, my hand caressing the spot where our baby has just moved.

I feel sad for Elias that he can't experience the pregnancy in the same way that I can. I mean it sincerely when I tell him, "Elias, I wish you could feel what I'm feeling."

He just smiles.

The faded red and deep-green bottle brush trees sway outside the buttercream-trimmed French windows. My mother-in-law is in high spirits. This weekend we are celebrating International Women's Day. We are in a familiar relaxed and slightly sleepy post-lunch state, after another plentiful and delicious meal.

"It's time for some coffee," Fifi announces with a mischievous smile, "but since we're celebrating women today, one of the men will make the coffee. It's our day, and we should relax."

"That's a great idea, Fifi," I respond, watching the bemused expressions of the rest of the family.

"You know that I taught my boys how to do everything. I wanted them to be able to take care of themselves, to be independent."

"I know, Fifi, and I thank you for this every day," I say, teasing her gently.

"So, how shall we do this? I know . . . we'll draw straws and whichever one of my boys picks the short one has to make the coffee."

Elias and his three brothers are smiling broadly. "Okay, let's do it," says my husband, always up for a challenge. Our niece, Elias's elder brother's daughter, a tween, looks terribly embarrassed. "Oh, I hope my papa doesn't have to do this," she half-prays under her breath, but loud enough that I hear her. I'm a little irritated by the fervor of her wish. What's so bad about having to make coffee for your family, anyhow?

But truth be told, in my almost seven years in Ethiopia, I've never once seen a man perform the coffee ritual. In Ethiopia it is simply referred to as "making coffee," or perhaps making *jebena* coffee—making coffee in the traditional clay pot. It is always a woman, or a girl, who sits on the low stool surrounded by family and neighbors.

It's Elias who gets the shortest straw. Without any comment, he starts gathering what he needs and setting up the brazier, the demitasse cups on the wooden stand that is for this specific purpose, and invites us to sit outside on the verandah looking onto our garden with bottle brush trees and a multitude of flowers that thrive in the temperate Addis Ababa climate.

As he starts the process of washing and then roasting the green coffee beans, my husband doesn't crack jokes about his coffee-making role, nor does he appear embarrassed in any way by it. As I've observed him in almost every other situation in our life together, Elias just gets on with the job at hand.

I turn to our niece. "See it's not so bad, he'll make great coffee."

Elias sits on a low stool and has placed some green grass and flowers around the setting. Nature's bounty—flowers and the lemlem green, verdant green—are always present at a coffee ceremony. First, he sorts the green coffee beans, making sure there are no small stones or anything else among them. Then he washes the beans, rinsing them three times in cold water. He places the wet, green coffee beans on a wide, round metal pan with a handle, which rests on a small charcoal stove. He lights some incense in a small dish reserved for this purpose. It's a combination of myrrh and frankincense and the smoke rises, mixing with the aromas of the newly roasting coffee. The embers are glowing, and he uses a long, curved metal utensil to move the beans around, occasionally simply shaking the pan to make sure they roast evenly. The beans get dark, and then they start to shine with their own oils. He lifts the metal pan and walks over to each one of us. We curve our palms and gently beckon the roasting aroma and appreciate the tantalizing smell of roasting coffee. Once he's offered everyone a chance to savor the smell, he returns to his stool and places the pan of beans down to let them cool. And he puts the black clay jebena with water onto the charcoal stove, to start to boil the water.

I'm mesmerized by the sight of all these steps that I have seen a thousand times being performed by a man. Elias is big-boned, and tall. And while he is efficient and graceful in his movements, this is such a contrast from the way I've watched Ethiopian women sitting on the low stool, gathering in their long white skirts and dresses, knees pressed together and slanted, sitting at a slight diagonal to the embers in front to them. Dainty wrists and slim arms, sitting at once as the center of attention and at the same time as a background to the conversations going on all around them.

Around us, our family is teasing Elias about how well he's making the coffee.

"Oh, I can't wait to taste this very special coffee," Fifi says with a twinkle in her eye.

Now Elias takes the beans, which in some households would be pounded in a wooden mortar, and instead takes them to our kitchen to grind them in our coffee grinder.

When he returns, he puts the ground coffee into the boiling water in the *jebena*. When the coffee is ready, Elias holds the *jebena* high and pours steaming dark liquid directly into the tiny cups without spilling a drop. Elias serves all the women first, starting with Fifi. As is traditional, he prepares a second round by adding water again to the jebena and then, finally, the blessings of the coffee in the third round, *baraka*.

We are in the same house, in the same living room, overlooking the front porch and the garden of verdant greens beyond, a kaleidoscope of flowers and bottle brush trees swaying gently in the afternoon breeze. This time, a dimple-thighed and still wobbly Juni is playing on my lap. My other mother-in-law, Elias's birth mother, Alem Gena, is staying with us. It has been an emotional visit, Elias getting to know his birth mother for the first time since he was a small child of four or five years old. I practice my Amharic with her every day but have trouble understanding her sometimes; I'm so used to the urban Addis-Ababa Amharic of my work colleagues and Elias's friends. Alem Gena lives in the countryside, and the difference in the lilt and intonation of her words is apparent even to me.

She holds out her arms for Juni, and I pass our baby to her grandmother. As seems to be the universal human custom, Alem Gena's voice changes to a higher pitch as she baby-talks with Juni and rocks her, exaggerating her own words and actions to draw a smile from my daughter.

I take the opportunity to get up, use the bathroom, and get a glass of water from the kitchen.

When I come back, the baby-talk is still going and has veered into a different direction.

"When you get bigger, you'll make the coffee . . . yes, yes, yes . . . yes you will. You will make the coffee."

"She's not even six months old," I say stiffly.

"Yes, but she's a girl, and soon she'll be a big girl, and girls make the coffee."

Anger rises in me. My cheeks feel hot. My child is a blank slate. I haven't even started to imagine her future roles. I know her grandmother is talking to her with love, but I am enraged in this moment. Growing up in Nepal, I had my share of being told what girls should and could do, and I've observed the same stultifying rigidity of gender roles in Ethiopia.

That night, Elias and I talk before bed. In the darkness, I say to him, "Elias, I don't want Juni to grow up with all these expectations about being a girl and what she can and can't do. I can't believe it's starting so early. She's just a baby. Anyhow, it's not about the coffee," I continue after a pause, "I love making coffee."

For all the pleasures of our privileged life in Addis
Ababa, there is no doubt that we live in a controlling
and authoritarian political system. We are careful in
sharing political opinions, and of criticizing the ruling
party or their decisions. So is everyone else that we
know. It is hard to know who to trust entirely, and too
easy to suspect when something is out of the ordi-
nary. Is the phone clicking simply because there is a
bad connection? Or is there something more sinister
at play? Gathering in public for political reasons is forbidden. Journalists are imprisoned, and independent
papers shut down by the government. In the absence
of information, speculation and rumors grow, and we
hear about violence in the far regions. Meanwhile, the
state television station reports on the ribbon-cutting
of the latest infrastructure project. We love our life
in Ethiopia, but we can't ignore what is all around us.

We decide to move to the US, where I have lived before, but Elias has only visited. We pick New York City deliberately. It's the city of dreams. I joke with Elias that after our move, he should join every single street protest in New York City, simply because he can.

Moving to the US is a big decision, one we come to after many late-night conversations. But it makes sense to me because, after Nepal, it's the country I have lived in longest, first as a scholarship student in Massachusetts, then a young professional in Washington, DC. In fact, I am a US resident, a green card holder. And Elias and I have particularly enjoyed New York on our previous visits there. Elias's business in Addis Ababa is doing well enough, but the potential for growth is limited. We are not optimistic that the political environment in Ethiopia will change for the better any time soon.

We tell ourselves it doesn't have to be a permanent move. We tell ourselves we can always come back.

There's so much to do. We will move from a house to an apartment, so have a considerable downsizing job to do with our belongings. The hardest decisions for me, as in every move of my life, is which books I keep and which ones I must let go. There are other preparations too. My job search in New York is pretty clear: my whole career since my first internship after college has been international nonprofit work, in health, education, water, and sanitation, and I'm looking for a professional role in New York in the same field. Elias, however, has been a serial entrepreneur. The last time he worked for someone else he was eighteen years old. He's done a bunch of different things, from running a taxi service to a delivery and logistics operation to a popular lunchtime crowd-pleasing restaurant. His first job ever was as a barista. We brainstorm together, and know that in New York too his entrepreneurial nature will be most suited to starting a business.

From our visits together to Asia, Europe, and the United States, Elias is keenly aware of the deep stereotypes about Ethiopia in the rest of the world. From the media spotlight on the terrible famines of the early 1980s, and the Live Aid and Band Aid concerts, there is a global memory of emaciated kids with flies in their eyes. But every time we host anyone who is visiting Ethiopia for the first time—friends, family, or work colleagues—they are taken aback and taken in by the beauty, history, and diversity of the country. This is not to discount the suffering caused by droughts and famines, but this explains why Elias feels strongly that any business he starts in the US should be rooted in a different narrative of Ethiopia. It doesn't take long for him to settle on coffee. Coffee permeates the daily life of Ethiopians like I've never seen it anywhere else. It's not just a product or a commodity, it has a deep history. It's a gift, a welcoming, a blessing. Coffee takes on whole words of meaning.

Legend has it that an Ethiopian goat-herder named Kaldi first discovered the coffee cherry. Coffee grew wild in the ancient forests of the Ethiopian plateau, and still grows wild in some parts of the country. The story goes that that Kaldi noticed that his goats became energetic and lively after they ate berries from a specific type of tree. When Kaldi brought some of these berries to the monks at the local monastery, and told them about his observations, the abbot ground up the berries, mixed them with butter, and made them into small balls. After the abbot ate his concoction, he noticed that he felt more alert and awake through long hours of praying at night. The word of the magical properties of the coffee cherry then spread to other monks and monasteries of the ancient Ethiopian Orthodox Church. There are historical discrepancies in this account, but it has taken hold as the most popular story around the discovery and origin of coffee.

While coffee has been all around us and a part of everyday life until this point, Elias now decides he must learn about it more formally. He starts his research and meets with coffee growers, cooperative leaders, exporters, and the considerable, deeply expert coffee community in Ethiopia. Two of our friends have deep roots in the coffee business community, and they are generous with their time and advice. We agree we will start exploring opportunities as soon as we landed in New York.

In our limited luggage allowance, Elias carefully packs his most special coffee beans. These are green—unroasted—beans, which in Ethiopian style he will carefully hand-roast and use as samples once we arrived in New York.

New York

"**I** WANT TO GO BACK HOME. What am I doing here?"

"Elias."

"I'm serious. I think we made a big mistake."

My husband is not the dramatic one in our relationship. And he's said the words that I have sensed in our first few weeks and months in New York City. I replay our old life in my mind. I know indulging in this self-pity-tinged nostalgia is probably not productive. I do it anyway. I'm pretty sure we have made a colossal mistake. One I'm not sure how to undo. And now, he's said it.

I am scared. I can't function in the tiny apartment. I slow down to a halt. There are long periods of being completely still, of feeling literally immobilized while my husband makes dinner or gives Juni a bath. I am there and not there, like being in a trance.

Now his words shake me awake, and I feel guilty. I think of everything that has completely changed for him. Even something as mundane as the weather. We left Addis in the cool, rainy season, but even the dry parts of the year are temperate due to the city's high altitude. We arrived in New York just in time for its steamy July and August, where the air is as still as a sauna. The first few days before we had air-conditioners were unbearably hot and humid. When Elias commented about the heat, our new neighbors would laugh: "But, you're from Africa, man!"

Elias understands English well, but is still hesitant in his responses, not fully confident using the language. He tries to explain that there are all types of climates in Africa, and in his country, Ethiopia, he grew up surrounded by mountains, where the air wasn't wet and steamy like this.

He has gone from his daily rituals of friendship, meeting at the local kebele for a beer with his friends, the regular rhythm of mutual support and community, helping out at a wedding or going to be with a friend at a funeral, to an emptiness—the three of us, Elias, Juni, and I, are in a kind of suspended reality, feeling the pressures of being overly reliant on each other, and having to be everything to each other.

Then there are the uncertainties. Even as we are meeting new friends and neighbors and discovering places, at the back of both of our minds, and Elias's most heavily, is the fact that he is here on a visitor's visa, and neither one of us has a job. This insecurity is like our own shadow, staying right beside us, us no matter how fast we walk.

I guess there are days when I get up and get out. I interview for jobs, I try to renew contact with old acquaintances, and I try to help my husband find his feet in this new city of millions. But there are days when it seems we have made a terrible mistake. When all the doors seem to be closed. We simply don't have the network of close friends and family who could make introductions for us and connect us to the skills and resources we need.

Elias still wants to start a coffee business. This will allow him to change from his visitor's visa to a category of visa for people coming to the US to engage in trade or business connected to their home country. We know the "E category" visa is a long shot, but it is our only shot. In Ethiopia, we have a lot of contacts, including some who are quite familiar with the intricacies of US immigration laws and visa types. But no one we know has heard of anyone who has successfully applied for an E visa.

We have no work, and we are relying on our savings, which at New York City prices are quickly evaporating. There is a chance that my husband, who is in the US on a perfectly valid visitor's visa, will nonetheless have to go back to Ethiopia when it expires. Our worries about what the future holds are with us every day. Still, we hold tightly to each other and to our optimism, perhaps baseless, that we will make it.

We search for a name for our business. We debate the pros and cons of various names, and practice saying lots of them, feeling them in our mouths and listening carefully to how each might sound to American ears, how each might be pronounced in American English. One late summer morning, we are all three walking down our block. Elias will drop Juni to the small family-run daycare where she has started to go for half-days, and I am on my way to meet an old acquaintance in the hopes that this meeting might turn up some leads for work, short or long term.

As we are walking down the block, I throw out a word that delights me: bunni. Bunni means brown in Amharic, and also plays on the word for coffee, bunna. We must spell it with an extra 'u' so that no one will pronounce it 'bunny'.

There is another reason it feels particularly appropriate. As we have met people in the specialty coffee world, attended our first trade show, and visited countless New York City coffee shops for research and pleasure, we have been struck by the absence of people from the countries where coffee is grown. To put it more bluntly, the specialty coffee scene (and the "hipster" coffee scene) in New York are strikingly white. We, on the other hand, are black and brown, and like the coffee, have grown and been nurtured on African and Asian soil. Naming our company Buunni is a counterpoint to the prevailing coffee culture that we observe. We decide on our company's name, and smile at our inside joke.

We begin to adjust to our new life in New York, which is at times in jarring contrast to the life we left in Addis Ababa. The sidewalks in our part of Manhattan smell like dog piss in the steaming muggy summer heat, and the smell only sharpens in the crisp fall and dry winter air. But we live near a gorgeous park—a hidden gem near the very top of Manhattan. Our walks in Fort Tryon Park are a physical relief from our cramped quarters, and the river views, the garden of all seasons, and the open expanses are a respite from the view from our own apartment windows— they look into other people's homes, and a brick wall.

We get to know many of our neighbors during our strolls in the Fort Tryon Park and the hours Juni spends in the two neighborhood playgrounds closest to us. These spaces offer an informal gathering place to meet other people in the community, parents, childcare providers, grandparents, and visiting relatives. We feel welcome and comfortable in these interactions.

Juni is social and curious and enjoys meeting friends at the playground. During our times there, people start up conversations with us easily. We are invited to birthday parties, picnics at the park, and playdates for Juni.

But raising children in New York is a different undertaking than in Ethiopia or Nepal. It feels like a far bigger, and lonelier, job, but also one that is oddly (to us) planned so much around the child. Infinite children's activities have parents and caretakers shuttling around the kid's "schedules." Where we come from, the idea that a small child might have a schedule elicits a giggle. I'm generalizing, of course, but raising a child in Elias's and my cultures is not the parent's job alone, and tends to be a communal endeavor supported by the extended family. It also is one that revolves more around the adults and adults' priorities rather than the child's.

But in our neighborhood, I also see similarities. In good weather, the playground is our new extended family of adopted relatives, friends, and neighbors. Parents chat and congregate by the respective age groups of their children. They form a New York version of the extended families and network of neighbors that Elias and I are familiar with from our own cultures. There the dark-circled, sleep-deprived crowd, the parents of infants (often longing for a good cup of coffee); there are others whose exhaustion is more physical, stemming from running after newly mobile toddlers, rescuing them from the latest near-calamity. We develop friendships that start at the playground but move beyond it, which will be particularly helpful during the long winter months.

By September of that year, I have a small consulting assignment with an international nonprofit. In October, I am offered a job with an international blindness-prevention organization. This is a huge relief. And in addition to having a regular income again, our whole family now has health insurance. I am baffled by the injustice and waste in the healthcare system in the US, which I had understood at an intellectual level before. These three months have given me much more personal insight into the lack of affordable healthcare.

How is the richest country on earth not able to provide healthcare to its people? I have worked on global health and health programs in developing countries, and have seen terrible conditions at health centers or clinics because of a lack of funds or trained staff—but in every case, the government was committed to trying to provide universal health care to all of its citizens. In the US, I am perplexed and saddened to see the opposite—a country with tremendous wealth and skills, but where millions of people do not have the security and dignity of basic health services. I also learn that in the US, somehow dental care and vision aren't included in many health plans.

While I'm relieved that for our family my new job provides the peace of mind of having good health insurance, I remain troubled by the fact that quality healthcare is a luxury and a privilege in America. Many of the indicators I've closely tracked in countries around the world, including maternal mortality rates, are going in the wrong direction in this country.

Looking back now, I am stunned at the precariousness of our position.

We discover that our new neighborhood has an all-volunteer-run annual Harvest Festival. This seems like the perfect opportunity to introduce our new community to Ethiopian coffee. We inquire about hosting a coffee table, and to our delight, we are welcomed enthusiastically.

Through the neighborhood email list, we find an exceptionally talented designer. Liz helps us create the visuals to give life to the business that Elias and I would like to create. We work with her on our logo, our first website, and an online shop—an identity for our baby business and an affirmation that it exists. I discover I love working with Elias and Liz to give shape to our amorphous, something-Ethiopian-coffee-related idea. It is a productive time: our limited resources force us to be persistent and creative.

Our neighborhood email list comes to our rescue again and again. It's how we know what's happening. My friend Sarah introduced me to the list while I was still in Addis, and with few contacts of our own, we rely on the listserv for information mainly relevant to parents with young children, but other topics, too. No question is too silly to ask, and there's always a patient person willing to take the time to explain a process or share their research. It is a true community resource, fueled by the generosity, resourcefulness, and entrepreneurialism of our neighbors. It is a lifesaver: an incredible selection of books for Juni are dropped off to our door, as are odds and ends to make our apartment more habitable. We also find names of local pediatricians, and introductions that prove to be essential for our business.

The day of the Harvest Festival, Elias and I have a plan. We will take turns staffing our table and running back to our apartment to make more coffee. We have a couple of carafes, and a home coffee maker. Elias has roasted the coffee in our kitchen and allowed it to breathe for a few days. We will grind the freshly roasted beans just before making the coffee.

It turns out to be a magical day. Crisp fall air, a spotless blue sky, sun on our faces, and conversations with our neighbors. People want to know more about the coffee, and our stories about coffee are about our families, our communities, our friends, and the coffee farmers. The Harvest-Festival-goers seem to delight in both the taste of our coffee and the tone of our stories.

"Hey, so is it true that Ethiopia is the birthplace of coffee?"

"Yes, it still grows wild in some of the forests—it's special coffee. In Ethiopia, coffee is so much more than just a commodity. It was the Yemenis and the Arab traders that introduced coffee to the world, but in Ethiopia, coffee is about family, and neighbors, and community. Like this. Like the Harvest Festival."

I watch Elias talk, and notice how much more confident he is already in his English. I enjoy watching his gestures becoming more animated, his hands moving as he speaks.

"In my culture, it's a bit weird to drink coffee alone. It's supposed to be shared, over conversation. It's a blessing. It's how you find out what's happening in your neighborhood, or town or country."

We brainstorm and argue, sometimes long into the night, in hushed tones, careful not to wake Juni. Our conversations mainly revolve around how to get around the latest obstacle in our path. That we are starting a business when there is no guarantee Elias will be allowed to stay in the US might seem like lunacy to some. To us, it is survival, and a hope that if we keep faith in ourselves and in this country, then we will make it. Our hope is fueled by action and love. We have fallen hard for the American Dream, even though we can see all around us evidence that the dream hasn't come true for so many.

Elias and I both grew up in countries with high rates of poverty, and we saw it every day. Yet there is something so unsettling about seeing poverty in the richest country in the world. Living in New York, we see people every day for whom there is no safety net. Those, who through one misfortune or another, have tripped and fallen into an abyss they cannot get out of.

There are dangers lurking around us, many scenarios of things going horribly wrong. Mercifully, our discipline and optimism are single-minded. We are going to make it. There is no other option.

One of our first steps is to apply for a business tax ID number. After we finish our online application, Elias asks me where we must take our printed confirmation. When I tell him the process is complete, and now we simply wait for the tax ID to arrive in the mail, he looks at me disbelievingly.

"Yes, but where do I have to take the document that arrives in the mail?"

"Nowhere, we keep it for our files and we use it when anyone asks for our Tax ID number."

"Are you sure?" he asks, unconvinced.

The following week, the document arrives. Elias is buoyant. "Unbelievable," he says. "In Ethiopia I would have had to go to a government office and spend hours waiting and maybe they would have told me to come back next week, just because they could." We delight at how easy and quick the administrative setup of a business is. We celebrate every single small accomplishment as evidence that we are moving forward.

Other days are tough. One of the things Elias desperately wants is to spend some time with an existing coffee business—to learn how things are done here in the US. He is keenly aware that while his own experiences will help him, that he needs US experience. He is not allowed to work as an employee, so he wants to volunteer. He works up his courage and asks a nearby coffeehouse and restaurant. He gets a lukewarm response. He asks me to help him with an email explaining our situation, reassuring the owner he won't be any trouble, that he isn't a competitor, and that he will even promise not to open a coffee-house within a certain distance. The silence is dis-heartening, and it feels like another closed door that we can't open.

We live these days very much like our toddler daughter. She walks unsteadily, inevitably falls, cries, and gets up again.

We are starting to get online orders, and Elias is delivering freshly roasted coffee on foot to custom-ers in our neighborhood. We bring Buunni to holiday markets, and show up at grassroots and community events, like our neighborhood clean-up day and the local Easter Egg hunt. Many of these events are run by volunteers, and the adults gratefully gravitate towards the coffee.

With my new job, I have a trip to Ethiopia and sev-eral other countries in Africa coming up. We decide to go as a family. It's wonderful to be back in Addis, and yet strange, too, not to be going back to our old home, not to be seamlessly stepping into the life we have left behind. Still, we are reunited with family and friends, we stop by our old haunts, and Elias connects with the coffee community in Ethiopia.

The conversations Elias has with coffee exporters in Addis makes it clear that we are not equipped to order at the scale they want. We aren't able to order the volume needed for a shipping container, and the costs of airfreight, which allows smaller quantities, is prohibitive. On top of this, we will have to figure out insurance and storage in the US. It's becoming clearer to us that the system is not set up for small (tiny) businesses like ours.

When we arrive back in New York, we are still determined, but the trip to Ethiopia has been sobering. One day, after picking Juni up from her daycare, Elias and I are walking up the quiet Pinehurst Avenue. Juni stops every five seconds to inspect something on the sidewalk.

"Sarina, look at this." Elias is pointing at a small, old storefront, a shoe repair shop we've walked by many times. This time there is a "For Rent" sign on the window, along with a phone number. "He must have gone out of business. Maybe while we were away."

"Should we call the number? Just to look."

"Yeah. I mean, I know we're not going to go into retail. It would be a pain, and a distraction."

"Though it would be great to be able to have a decent cup of coffee in the neighborhood."

"Maybe there are others like us." I can see it. A coffee shop. Right here. It would be perfect.

"Yeah, I'm not sure that's a great reason to open a coffee shop! But, let's call."

"We're only looking."

"Yup. Only looking."

It turns out that the broker for the space is the small, independently owned real estate brokerage directly opposite the shoe repair shop space. We get an appointment to see the place the very next day. When we walk in, it's dark and dirty inside, with layers of grime, but there are sweet little miniature figures lined up on the window. And there are other little touches, like the small, shoe-shaped wind chime that hangs in a corner. The space is deep and narrow, like many old spaces in the city. Unusually, it has a skylight, but it's been covered with metal bars that give it a prison-like feel.

"Look at these ceilings!"

"Look at the walls."

"It has potential."

"Definitely."

"How much is the rent?"

That very evening, I start working on our application for the space. I know it's a long shot, because we don't have business track record in the US. While Elias has a lot of small business and entrepreneurial experience, somehow we know it doesn't "count" the same way as if he'd had a business in New York City. I put all my energy and creativity into the application.

I write a post on the neighborhood email list, and ask how would people feel about a coffee shop in the now-vacant shoe repair shop. I reach out to local parents, business owners, and others we've gotten to know in the area and ask them to write letters of recommendation. I write up a description of what our future coffee shop will be like, and why there's a market for it in the community. I print out and attach all the email list-serve responses to my coffeehouse proposal. I put together our resumes, and bank statements, and character references. I review it three times before I hand it over to the broker.

A couple of days later, we get a call. The landlord wants to meet us. He selects a kosher deli in midtown. Elias and I are thrilled. We know that if he wasn't considering us, he wouldn't ask to meet and waste his time. On the subway on our way to midtown, we hold hands and talk softly.

"It will be fine."

"Yeah, what's the worst that can happen?"

"That they say no. They won't say no. Why would they meet us to say no? Remember to tell them about your restaurant in Addis."

"I will."

"It will be fine."

"Deep breaths. They will love us." Now I've made both of us laugh.

When we get to the deli, there are two men sitting at a table, and the younger one gets up to greet us. He introduces us to his uncle. As soon as we say our hellos, I notice the twinkle in the older man's bright blue eyes. We're prepared for their questions. The main one is if we're sure we can make money selling only coffee.

I feel that our conversation is going well. "We wanted to meet you. Eye to eye. But my wife, she really liked your application. She said we should let you have the space." The older man's eyes are warm, and I beam back at him.

We celebrate our one-year-anniversary in New York city by moving to a two-bedroom apartment. It's a block away from the dollhouse where the three of us have been sleeping on a huge mattress on the floor. Our new apartment is sun-drenched and gorgeous, but our first morning, I am awake at dawn listening to the sounds of the garbage trucks, the buses, the cars and car alarms, and of course, the sirens. Pros and cons, I think to myself.

We are about to open Café Buunni in the old shoe-repair shop. The hanging shoe windchime is now in the basement, a reminder of the space's past. In these final weeks of construction, Elias is busy as always with our Chinese contractor. He jokes that he is starting to understand Chinese. He spends every day with them, not just overseeing but helping, and chatting as they all eat Chinese takeout lunch from the restaurant on the corner.

One afternoon, as we often do, Elias and I are standing outside the brown-paper-covered window at 213 Pinehurst Avenue. There are no benches yet, so we stand and gaze at the storefront, imagining what the future might hold for us. This afternoon, we are here with our star intern, Bea. Bea is an undergraduate at Barnard College, and one of the most talented and creative people I have ever met. She's a hard worker, and a pleasure to work with. I would hire her in a heartbeat. She designed our coffee gift cards and our "Coming Soon" poster that's on the window. Now we're talking about the sign outside our soon-to-be coffee shop. Bea thinks she can make the sign with stencils and gold spray paint, and I love the idea of a home-made sign.

As we're chatting, a woman I don't know stops in front of us.

She looks directly at Bea. "Hi! So excited about this place. Is it your place? When's it opening?"

Bea looks embarrassed. "Um, actually, Sarina and Elias here are the owners," she gestures towards us.

The woman turns to us, slightly taken aback. "Oh. Hi! Well, good luck. We're excited."

It's a small moment. This conversation that lasts barely two minutes. I don't remember the woman's face anymore. But I have never forgotten this interaction. Bea was seventeen years old. And Elias and I were standing right there.

On September 14, 2012, fourteen months after our arrival in New York, we open Café Buunni.

We think we are prepared. Elias traveled to attend a training about retail specialty coffee to learn more about American coffee culture, tastes, and market. The training was in Portland, Oregon, run by the kind and talented people at the American Barista and Coffee School. We read how-to books, scoured the Internet for resources, and eagerly soaked in the overwhelming array of information and products at the Coffee Fest trade show at the massive Javits convention center in New York City. With help from the Coffee School, we created detailed spreadsheets with our business projections.

Elias stood on the sidewalk of Pinehurst Avenue with a clicker adding up the number of people walking by at different times of day. We interviewed staff in our living room and on-boarded them with our Ethiopia-inspired coffee philosophy. One thing we reiterated with our team was respect for the coffee itself and for the farmers who grew it. Respect for the bean informs our many decisions from the start. It's why our coffees comes from small farms in Ethiopia, why we buy from farmers' cooperatives, how we select our roaster, and we want our team to understand this. Elias stresses that the beans our baristas are grinding have passed through at least twenty pairs of hands treating them with care and love, so that when we are preparing our drinks, we are confident that we are using the top 10% of all coffee in the world.

Someone hand-picked the seventy cherries that go into your one cup of coffee. You have to respect that. If you love coffee, you have to love the people who grow it, who care for it, who allow you to experience that "aahh" first sip of a truly great cup. We are proud of our coffee, but we are also stewarding it in its journey from seed to plant to cherry, as it's picked by hand, washed and processed, or sundried and carefully sorted. Roasted just right. And here it is in our hands, right before we prepare it for the customer's cup. It's a big responsibility. Don't mess it up.

I feel the thump of my heart. I stand behind the cash register, my genuine beaming smile becoming tight and uncomfortable as I work as fast as I can. Yet the line keeps growing until I can't see the end. People line up out the door and around the corner of the block. I remind myself to keep breathing, and focus as best as I can on the person in front of me, trying to contain my growing panic.

The only other personal experience I can relate these first few days and weeks after our opening to is the birth of Juni. Sleep-deprived, overwhelmed, wondering oh-my-god-what-have-we done, and moments of pure, piercing pride and joy.

On our second evening, as we are starting to close up the shop, Greg walks in. He is a familiar face in the neighborhood, and at this time a casual acquaintance. Someone we say hi to if we pass each other walking down the street.

"How's it going?" His smile is warm.

We respond politely in our exhaustion. Maybe he sees our joyous pride on our faces, or maybe he sees how overwhelmed we are. I hope for the former.

"I made some stew, and I brought you guys dinner. I figured you're busy."

I stare at him, then glance over at Elias. "Thank you," I say. "Thank you. This is the perfect gift."

We learn every day, on the go. We are humbled by the people lining up to try out our coffee. They compliment us on the transformation of the space, they rave about the quality of our coffee, admire the artistry of our baristas, and most importantly, they show up every day. There are rough edges for sure, and maybe there will always be, but in the first days after opening our doors, it is clear that our tiny little space has filled an unmet need, and that we can count on the support of our neighbors.

We have blown through our projections, and don't have time to update the spreadsheets. While everyone comments what a good problem it is to have, we have to think on our feet, find new suppliers, place urgent orders, and make frequent runs to our local supermarket. There are glitches and crises aplenty. The water pressure is too low and is causing problems with the espresso machine. We run out of what we thought was a week's supply of coffee beans during our opening weekend. We have to change milk suppliers within the first few weeks. Some of our team members have other plans and dreams, and rightly leave us to pursue them.

As we spend time talking to customers in our shop, we understand that they expected the quality of the coffee and the pastries to be good, but that there are many intangibles as to why they keep coming back. I beam to my husband, "Elias, we have regulars!"

After three months, the numbers are looking good, and six months after opening our business, we break even. This is something almost unheard of in our industry. Lucky for us, Juni is a social and easy-going toddler. During our opening months, she spends many hours in a patchwork of care. Parents we have gotten to know at the playground, at her daycare, our friend Sarah, and the occasional babysitter all care for and watch over her, bathe her and feed her. Bone-tired as we are, we are happy. From the start, for us, Buunni was a labor of love: it is our good fortune that our community loves us back.

"It's like a hug," says Melody. "I've met so many people here. If you hadn't put this big, long community table here, I don't know if we'd all be talking, but we do. You kind of have to. It's like being at a dining table."

"There's community in the air, in the atoms here . . . in the physicality of the space," Rita muses. We're waiting for Julia, the neighborhood pharmacist extraordinaire. It's Tuesday night writing group. There have been other iterations: There was a knitting club. And that was mainly young moms or moms to be, and it had a very different energy. But the writers are a diverse group. There's generally one man who shows up. A different one each time. And a group of women ranging from forty to sixty. What is that age group now? Is it called middle-aged? These are women who've seen a bunch of things, and done a bunch of things, who are smart and have things to say, and things to write. And I'm here with them. It's delightful to realize that I'm now one of these women I describe.

I wake up feeling nauseous. I gag before I've even put the toothbrush in my mouth. I remember this feeling, and as horrible as it is, I smile a little smile to myself. I'll wait for a few days. Maybe it's nothing. Suddenly I'm doubled over the sink, retching. I haven't closed the bathroom door, and Juni wanders in looking worried.

"Mama's sick, Papa! Mama's sick in the bathroom!"

So much for waiting a little while.

"It's okay, sweetheart. Mama's fine." She's hugging me around my legs as I take deep breaths and reassure her while trying to breathe myself out of the overwhelming nausea. We need to fix the bathroom lock.

"What's going on? Are you okay?" Elias looks worried and gently pries Juni from my legs.

"Let's give Mama a little bit of space, sweetheart. Are you okay?"

I smile wryly at him. "Yes, I'm okay. Just very nauseous."

He raises his eyebrows, and his eyes search my face. "What kind of nauseous?" A slight smile starts to play on his lips. "*That* kind of nauseous?"

I start to answer, then just nod my head and bend over the sink again.

We have an opportunity to apply for a holiday market at Bryant Park. It's a wonderful chance for Buunni to be known beyond our immediate neighborhood, and we eagerly complete the application and the in-person interview. Elias is worried we might be taking too much on, since our second child is due in late November, but I'm excited about this opportunity and don't want to pass it up.

Marte, a Norwegian friend of ours from the neighborhood, helps us build a beautiful booth for Buunni. She's strong, talented, and creative; she can build things, and uses power tools. In her professional role, she's a set designer for theater, but she's also an artist and artisan. I'm a little bit awestruck.

Thanks to Marte and Elias, we have a beautiful booth, and I help recruit and schedule staff for the booth, and then we're ready to go. It turns out to be an unseasonably cold fall and winter. As we go back and forth from our neighborhood at the top of Manhattan to Bryant Park near the middle of the island, I notice that the Hudson River largely appears to be frozen over. In our few winters here, we have never seen this.

I'm increasingly pregnant, feeling slow and uncomfortable. I can't sleep well, so I'm tired during the day. Our baby, who we've decided to call Maya, is due on the fifteenth of November, and we figure this gives us a couple of weeks to settle in with her before the market goes into full swing right after the Thanksgiving holiday. But Maya seems comfortable, and the days pass with no signs of labor. Juni, normally an easy-going and easy child, is cranky and clingy, and because it is so cold outside, we are spending most of our time indoors or driving between Washington Heights and Bryant Park, finalizing our booth, solving the latest problem, or filling in for someone who didn't show up or isn't feeling well. The booth is too cold for the staff, so we must buy temporary heaters, and the market is slow, partly because it's so unseasonably cold.

A few days after my due date passes, my doctor calls me to tell me that she's not comfortable waiting much longer.

"Other than being tired, I'm feeling fine. And the baby looks fine too."

"I know. Everything is fine, but the longer we wait the more there is a chance of complications. We have a few more days, but we can't wait indefinitely."

"What do you suggest?"

"Try walking. Go for long walks. It'll be good for you anyway."

I have a wonderful doctor who works with midwives in her practice. I've been seeing the midwives, and have had no complications so far. With Juni, my labor started a couple of weeks early, but I was able to experience a natural birth with no complications. I am really hoping for the same this time.

A week passes, and I'm feeling the pressure of the medical establishment, in addition to the pressure of my huge belly. I'm short of breath, my back aches, and it's impossible to get into a comfortable sleep at night. I'm avoiding calls from my doctor and going on long walks instead.

That night, after Juni falls asleep, I feel the first twinge. I've had a false alarm earlier in the week, so I deepen my breath and start organizing our room. There's another twinge, a stronger one this time. I look at my phone and write down the time. As I'm clearing up papers, putting away clothes, and keeping myself busy, I have an unmistakable contraction. Wow that was fast. They just started. That was a strong one. I better call Elias. And Rama. Okay. Deep breaths.

I call Rama first, as she's farther away. She will spend the night at our apartment with Juni while Elias and I are at the hospital. Then I call Elias, who is around the corner at Buunni. He's home within minutes. I'm pacing in our bedroom, taken by surprise at how fast things seem to be moving. Some time later, Rama arrives. The car ride to the hospital is almost unbearable. I feel every bump in the road, and curse the lack of investment in infrastructure.

"Elias, after taking her time, this baby is in such a hurry." I'm panting. Barely able to speak. Everything is happening to fast. This is not how I remember it. I can't keep up with the contractions, and I'm starting to feel scared.

When we get to the hospital, my midwife, Sabine, is there. She takes a look at me and starts to move fast.

"We need a room!" I hear her shouting, but it's as if she's very far away.

There's a loud noise. Boom! I'm startled.

"What's happening?"

"It's okay. Shhh . . . it's okay, it's just your water. It literally burst."

"We need a room, NOW."

Sabine guides me to a wheelchair. I look at her dumbfounded. I can't possibly sit. There's no way I can sit down in that thing. I'm holding Elias's hand with all my strength. Somehow I'm in the chair and they are running, wheeling me into a room. There's no time, I'm pushing and clenching, I can't hear anyone, only the pain that keeps building, and now I'm being split apart, and my insides are burning, and then with a final push, there is the sweet relief.

There's a flurry of activity in the room. I'm shaking and struggling to catch my breath, finally crying and reaching for my baby and for Elias.

The next day, Elias brings Juni to visit Maya and me in the hospital. My heart aches when I see Juni's face; she looks scared and hesitant. When she finally comes closer, I can tell she wants to get into the bed with me. I hug her and draw her in close. I watch her, watch her little sister. I remember the first time I saw my own little brother and my mom in the hospital. I wonder what Juni will remember of this day, later when she grows up.

"Why is she so pink? I didn't think she would look like this, Mama."

They spend an hour or so with us, and by the time they leave, the scared look has finally left Juni's face.

Just as Maya and I come home from the hospital, in those early days when nights and days blur into one, the market at Bryant Park is picking up. Elias is driving back and forth, replenishing supplies. There's no parking there, so most days I bundle Maya up and take her with us so she and I can be in the car while Elias loads and delivers the coffee supplies to the booth. I sit at the wheel with the blinkers on, and Elias works as fast as he can. Juni and Maya are in their car seats in the back. Invariably, Maya wakes up and starts wailing during these double-parked moments. I sit at the wheel as long as I can bear it, then I move to the back of the car to hold her and nurse her. Juni is confused and ill-tempered about these trips in the dark.

"What are we doing? How much longer will it take? Why are we stopping here? Can I go with Papa?" Her questions are incessant. I need to change Maya's diaper. Again.

I hear a knock on the window and look up to see a police uniform, and eventually, when I roll down the window, I see it's a policewoman.

"We'll just be a few more minutes. I have to change her diaper."

She looks at us, taking in the situation. I can't read her expression. "Okay. Take your time," she says finally, sounding almost sympathetic.

I breathe a sigh of relief. Then, I'm suddenly angry at the whole situation. What are we doing here sitting in the car with a newborn and a toddler, when we should be home? This is ridiculous. Is it worth it? For what? And in that moment, I just want my own Mama.

Somehow, we weave seamlessly between the logistics of our family life and the logistics of business. I know some couples who work together try to create boundaries and structure when business ends and personal life begins, but for us it's all mixed in together. It's the only way we know, and somehow it works. We look at Buunni's logo refresh while the kids are in the bath; we discuss what the month's numbers look like while Elias makes weekend French toast breakfast for all of us. Buunni is personal. It's something we have created together, that we're fiercely proud of, and so it's allowed in the kitchen, in the living room, and in the bedroom, just like our kids are. This doesn't mean we don't argue about it. Increasingly, our arguments are mild, and mostly occur because we take shortcuts when there is not enough time or patience to explain what we're actually trying to say. An unrushed conversation holds the magic key for us, and when we can manage that, all is well in our world.

Our skills and strengths are remarkably complementary, and we respect each other's expertise, and generally, with a few exceptions, stay out of each other's way. Elias is a numbers guy. The kind who can figure them out in his head. I can work things out methodically, thinking the steps on an Excel spreadsheet. When I arrive at my number, it's one he came up with quickly in his head at the beginning. After a lifetime in the international non-profit sector, owning a small business is the first time I've worked on something that is supposed to make a profit.

I get to work on what I consider the fun stuff: creative, communications, community engagement, and increasingly trying to build in social impact so that it's embedded in our business as it grows. Buunni's aim is not only to make a profit, but to contribute positively to our community, including our staff, and to not harm the planet. How completely I enjoy working on growing our tiny business has come as a delightful surprise to me.

Becoming American

THE DAY I GET MY US CITIZENSHIP, I am not one of those taking celebratory selfies in front of Federal Plaza. I don't have family members with flowers. My decision to come alone is deliberate. I haven't made the decision to become a US citizen lightly or quickly. When the day comes, I feel a keen sense of loss. I am formalizing the distance to my homeland, and the emotions that came with that, even after all these years, take me by surprise.

With my naturalization certificate safely in a folder in my bag, I walk unseeingly past many city blocks, my face wet with tears. It has been a journey of many years, numerous forms and fees, years of uncertainty and sacrifice. I've paid for the privilege of becoming a US citizen, and I know I won't take for granted the rights and responsibilities that this privilege comes with. I am prepared to be an informed and engaged citizen; I am looking forward to it.

I apply for a US passport. As a regular international traveler, I particularly savor the thought of getting on a plane, showing up at an airport in another country, paying twenty dollars, and being afforded the luxury of a "visa on arrival." I go to apply for my US passport at the Post Office near Grand Central Station in New York. The postal worker, a black woman with amber-brown eyes and a warm voice, interrupts me just as I'm beginning to explain all the documents that I have in my file.

"Honey, I know you got all your paperwork in order. You gave up the world to be here."

My eyes sting with the truth in those words. Not just me, but the countless millions of others, who, like me, have made sacrifices small and large to be here.

I have become a US citizen just in time to fully participate in the 2016 election cycle. I will vote at every opportunity I have, from my local state primaries to the national primaries and of course, the presidential elections. I research the candidates. I take participating in the political process seriously, perhaps even a little too earnestly.

In early 2016, as the presidential primary race is unexpectedly heating up, I find out that Bernie

Sanders is visiting New York and will be holding a rally in the Bronx. I offer to stay home with our two young daughters so Elias can attend. I am excited for Elias to attend as many public rallies and protests as he can, because public gatherings of this type were forbidden in Ethiopia.

Elias and I are both increasingly intrigued by the senator from Vermont, and he's going to be just a few miles from our home in Northern Manhattan. As I read more about the rally, I learn that Bernie is the first national-level politician to hold an event in the Bronx since John F. Kennedy. Apparently the Bronx is not at the top of the list for most politicians, though they visit New York on a regular basis.

Excited and energized after the rally, my Ethiopian husband asks me, "Why do people keep talking about the white 'Bernie-bros'? I didn't see that at all! There were all kinds of people." He reports that he saw a diverse crowd of different age groups and races, and tells me that the excitement was palpable and electric.

Bernie's plain-spoken, finger-wagging message feels so authentic. It resonates with us. I do joke with my friends that I wish for a candidate with Bernie's policy platform and Marco Rubio's demographics. But because Bernie is such an unlikely American politician, so genuinely himself, I feel a trust that I haven't felt for a very long time—maybe ever—with any other candidate. One night, Maya is finishing the last of her dinner. Sitting in her high chair with a large part of her evening meal spread around her face, a sleepy and cranky Maya complains, "But I want to go see Bernie Sanders!"

Having grown up overseas, Senator Sanders's political analysis and policy positions align with my beliefs and values, and with what I've seen in my own life, my work, and my extensive global travels. But in New York, including in my own district, it is clear which candidate is favored by the Democratic Party establishment, and it is not Bernie Sanders. At first I'm a little shocked at the clear favoritism displayed in New York. And as I learn more, I find out that New York has a history of political corruption, an old boys' network, and an entrenched party machine that is strong and seems impenetrable.

Despite an unexpectedly strong showing, Bernie loses the Democratic primary to Hillary, and she becomes the Democratic candidate for president. At the state level, the young Latina woman I vote for in the New York State Senate primaries wins her election as a progressive Democrat. Then I am stunned when she joins a group that caucuses with the Republican party to give them a majority in the State Senate. In return, she and this group, called the Independent Democratic Conference, get fancy offices, to chair committees, and receive money for their campaigns. I have a lot to learn about New York politics. But the more I learn, the less I like. This is what I am learning.

The mood at Buunni on Election Day is jubilant. There's a hum in the air. Customers are smiling; tips are good. People are treating themselves to a sweet to go along with their cappuccinos and lattes. The anticipation in our neighborhood of electing the first female president is palpable. We are making history. People are planning parties, buying supplies. At our local wine store, I run into a regular customer who tells me, "I was going to buy champagne, but then I thought, I don't want to jinx it, so I'll just buy lots of wine. We'll have time for champagne later." Another woman posts on our neighborhood email list, "Should we all gather outside after the election results? I know it will be late tonight, and kids will be sleeping, but we should do something to mark and celebrate this momentous occasion."

To someone like me, a candidate like Donald Trump could be from a different planet. I am confused that he isn't disqualified from running. Surely there are some minimum thresholds in order to be considered a candidate for the highest office in the country? I also don't understand why he is given a free platform and so much air-time and "oxygen," so much space in the public debate. Why is his message being amplified and repeated on every news channel, and every printed paper? I honestly don't understand, but as angry as I am about the campaign and candidate, I am not worried about the election.

We invite a few friends over to our apartment, and as we are watching the results start to come in, it becomes clear that it will be a very long night. We all have work the following day, so our friends go home, and eventually I go to bed.

The first thing I notice as I get on the subway car is the silence. I look around me and am met with eye contact. More people catch my eye and exchange a brief moment with me on this morning's subway ride than in my entire five years in New York City. Near me, an older woman shakes her head slowly, in silent disbelief, or perhaps disapproval. At the next stop, among the people who enter is a red-faced young woman who looks like she's just stopped crying and is trying hard not to start again. I sit down at a newly empty seat. My eyes are gritty from too little sleep. From my stop at the top of Manhattan, the train is speeding down the island, taking us, mostly morning commuters, to our places of work. I last five stops, and as the train pulls up to Columbus Circle/59th Street, the tears I have been holding back spill down my face.

It is the morning of Wednesday, November 9, 2016, and those who did not stay up late into the night are waking up to the fact that Donald Trump has won the US presidential election. Our neighborhood and our city and many parts of the country are in the very first stages of a real and collective grief.

How am I going to explain this to my kids? I can barely make sense of it. What lessons will they take from this? Maya is too young, but Juni is bright and she's paying attention. And someone who doesn't care about kids like her is going to be the president of the United States. My child, who once when she was three and we were watching the news shouted out to her parents and grandparents, "Look guys, the president! The president looks like Papa!"

Thoughts continue to race in my mind. Thank God we live in New York City, at least I don't have to worry about her in school and in the neighborhood. At least all of us are safe here. New York is an immigrant city, a sanctuary city, but my heart aches for other brown immigrant families and children and the very real fear they must be feeling. I think of my parents, stuck in limbo while they wait for their green cards. I think of Maria at the laundromat around the corner. Her heartbreak when her dad died has been made so much worse by the fact that she can't go to Mexico for his funeral. She is afraid of not being allowed back into the country she has made her home, but which has not yet welcomed her fully.

The splinters in my heart are for all of us.

America has elected a person who makes his contempt for us—people of color and immigrants—a loud and powerful part of his platform. And America has chosen him over us.

My voice sounds tight and strained. "Sometimes the side that we are rooting for doesn't win, Juni. Sometimes we lose. And it's disappointing and it feels awful. But we still go on believing and doing what we can. We don't give up on what we believe." I believe what I'm saying, but I want to burst into tears at the same time. I am trying my best to hold it together.

"But a lot of kids are sad, Mama. In my school only one kid said he would vote for Donald Trump. Most of the kids say they would vote for Bernie and Hillary."

"J, kids don't vote," I say in my distraction.

"I know, I'm just saying if we could vote, that's who we would vote for," she says, impatient that I haven't understood her.

How did young people vote? What would happen if the voting age was sixteen? Who didn't vote? I know this conversation with my daughter is important. That at almost seven years old, this might be one of those "forever memories" that she will remember later in life. But I am still too distraught and distracted myself. I do the best I can, and tell myself we'll talk about it again.

Juni is an observant and astute kid. In our family we joke about her "elephant ears." A few hours, or perhaps even a few days after Elias and I have had what we think is a private conversation, about a grown-up subject, Juni will refer to some aspect of that conversation. During the 2016 election campaign season, she hardly needed her elephant ears. The conversations were loud and clear, and the messages came from multiple sources and directions. We were careful in how much news we watched before the kids went to bed, but nonetheless, the blaring of the Donald Trump campaign was everywhere: "Mexicans are Rapists! We're going to build a wall! Grab them by the pussy!" The headlines in print and on the news were deteriorating beyond belief.

I am angry it has been allowed to get this far. Where are the grownups? The reasonable people in American politics? How far are they going to let this go? I am even more frustrated because I have gone through the US immigration process. I had an FBI background check; I was finger-printed; I had medical tests, the results of which were sealed and sent directly to the US government; I had to submit five-plus years

of tax returns. My birth certificate, marriage certificate, and divorce decree were all deemed highly
relevant to the process of getting a green card and
eventually becoming a US citizen. I had been vetted.
And I expect a candidate for president to be vetted at
least as much as I had. No. As someone applying to be
the leader of this country (I cringe when Americans
call their leader the "Leader of the Free World."
There is something so blatantly over the top, lacking
in any sense of perspective, history or humility in that
statement), I expect him to be vetted more.

I have other reasons to be angry too. My seven-
year-old has asked me a question, which I blame
squarely on our president: "Mama, what are rapists?"

These weeks are difficult. I'm an agile person; I enjoy
change and variety and being challenged. Having
traveled from a young age, I know myself to be
adaptable and flexible. But I have trouble adjusting
to the new political landscape in this country, and it
feels personal. I can't actually comprehend what has
happened. I try to think logically, but I find myself
just shaking my head. I can't understand what has
happened, and nor do I want to. And therefore, I'm

having trouble moving on to the next steps of deciding what my response should be.

I keep thinking it's a mistake, and even when
I know it isn't, I still hope something will change
the outcome. As the votes are counted, it becomes
clearer that most Americans did not vote for him.
Still, the country elected him president. It makes me
furious that America, with its confusing and ultimately undemocratic electoral college system, has
been sending teams of "election monitors" and passing judgment on elections all over the world. I am not
alone in my confusion and despair; I am surrounded
by it on the subway, at Buunni, at work, and in late-
night conversations with my husband after the kids
go to bed.

These days I often think back to the excitement
of the primaries. Some of us were so inspired by
Bernie's message, others on the verge of celebrating
America's first woman president. Despite my fondness for Bernie's platform, when the time came, and
he was not on the ballot, I voted for Hillary Clinton.
This is something I thought most women would do.

Before the presidential elections, many of my
friends overseas, perplexed by what they were seeing
on their own news channels, asked me when I traveled, "What do you think? What's going to happen?"

"If women turn out to vote, and they always do,
then Donald Trump will lose," I would say.

I was horribly wrong, of course. Women did vote—many, many white women voted for Donald Trump. 61% of white women without a college degree, and 45% of white college-educated women, to be precise. Significant percentages of upper and middle-class white women voted for Donald Trump. He couldn't have won without them. That stings the worst.

At first, I simply don't know what to make of this. Now I understand that that racism and misogyny in the United States are far more entrenched, and form a deeper and wider sea, than I had ever imagined. Now I know that they are powerful motivators.

Ugh. More gray hairs. It hasn't even been ten days since I colored my hair. All those chemicals. What's the point of eating organic when I'm dumping chemicals on my head every two weeks? And the expense!

I've been thinking about stopping my hair-coloring routine. On my mom's side of the family, everyone is prematurely gray. I've had grey hair since my twenties and now don't even know what my hair would look like without the color. Is it going to be all white? Salt and pepper? Annoyingly, the front my hair, all around my forehead, is where the grey seems most determined. If I just let it grow, I'd look like a zebra, so the only solution is to cut my hair short and let my naturally fast-growing hair grow out to whatever color is underneath decades of hair dye.

Meg, my Japanese hairdresser, checks with me again. "Are you sure? You are still too young, and your hair is so long. Cut it all off? Are you sure?"

"I'm sure. I'm so tired of doing something I don't believe in."

"Okay, then. I'm going to give you a fantastic haircut."

As she gets to work, long streaks of dark hair fall to the ground and on the plastic draped around my shoulders. I feel the thrill of freedom, of newness. Of looking in the mirror and seeing someone different.

At New York prices, I know I'm going to save a lot of money by not coloring my hair. I know already what I'm going to do with the money. I will start a monthly recurring donation to the ACLU, my small contribution to counter the ugliness I know is coming. Elias and I recently became proud "card-carrying" members of the ACLU. I will also put some of my hair-color money into a college savings account for our daughters.

When Meg is done, I pick up my dad from the iconic New York Public Library on 5th Avenue where he has been happily browsing. We walk through mid-town. There's a chill in the air, but it's not too cold—a mild November day. We walk to join in with the crowds of people gathering. There are young kids on their parents' shoulders—small, tired legs and a better view—there are older people, and young people, there are people of all shades and colors, different dress codes, and some have signs, and some don't. Some are chanting, some aren't. It's a New York City protest against the president, elected but not yet even sworn in.

"I was a young academic. It was a hopeful and revolutionary time. We protested against the Vietnam War. We protested against apartheid. I remember one of the chants: 'Hey, hey, LBJ, how many kids have you killed today?'"

I've heard these stories before. But I listen more attentively now. I feel attuned to my dad's experience in a different, closer way; I'm aware of the cyclical nature of life, of history, of politics. We are in a distinct political moment, but one that is connected to and rooted in the one he is describing. I feel a rush of gratitude that I have my dad by my side today.

As a new American, I have whole-heartedly adopted the slogan "Dissent is Patriotic." Dissent feels like my only salvation. But the weeks after the inauguration pass painfully slowly. We joke that this presidency is passing in dog-years; a Trump year is the equivalent of seven human years.

The confluence of technology, digital communications, and social media activism is captivating to me. Particularly for someone with my grueling schedule and business travel, it allows me to take part in a way that I wouldn't be able to do in person. I wake up and send a text, which a bot turns into a paper fax or an email that is delivered to my senator's and congressmen's office. And then I go to work. Or some days, then I brush my teeth. The every-day routine of activism makes me feel purposeful, the master of my task list. There is a spring in my step on the fax, petition, tweet, call days. And they become a regular part of the landscape of my day.

This is a novel experience for me. I've never felt that I had a political voice, or that anyone represented me. As a teenager, I left home right when Nepal started on its tumultuous and ill-fated journey towards multi-party democracy. For many years I was in a temporary status in the US: a student visa led to a one-year, practical training work visa, which led to a job offer and an employment-based visa, and over ten years after I first arrived in the US as a student—landing at JFK Airport, as so many do—I finally got my green card. But I filed taxes starting in my first year in the US, and have paid taxes ever since. I paid into social security, a vague concept to me at the time. I paid federal, state, and local taxes. Still, I had no representation. No voting, no elections, no calls nor letters. No one to hear my voice. And my gaze was therefore safely distant—no matter how many years I lived here, I refused to call it home. Not because of any ill-will towards America. But simply because I was still an outsider. I owned the official title "resident alien" that I was given as a green-card holder.

As a resident alien, I had the right of a certain distance. I didn't own the Iraq war. I didn't own disastrous US foreign policy. I didn't own what Americans still refuse to fully acknowledge as the genocide of the first nations, the indigenous people of this country. I didn't own slavery, or the civil rights movement, or the political decay, or money in politics. It existed, but it was not mine. I could critique and criticize, but I was not obligated to do anything about it because it really wasn't my problem. There were bigger problems in the world: HIV/AIDS was devastating a whole generation of people in the prime of their life. So many kids weren't able to get a decent education, and there was a global water and sanitation crisis. That was the world I focused on and wanted to make an impact on.

People around the world have an idea of America. It's the ultimate brand. Having grown up overseas, I know that. I remember my delight arriving in New York at the age of eighteen, seeing the swarms of yellow cabs and sidewalks full of aggressive speed-walkers on their way to their jobs. All of this was strangely familiar to me from the many American movies I'd watched. I'd arrived.

But my Hollywood-fueled impressions of the country were jolted the first time I saw a tall, thin, unwashed man reach into a garbage can on the street corner and fish out a half-eaten slice of pizza. He started to eat it right there, and I stared at him, my mind having trouble processing what my eyes were clearly seeing right in front of me.

I lived in the US, I paid taxes in the US, and I had American friends of various backgrounds. I even interacted with their parents, and in some cases, their whole extended families. Yet, always as an outsider. I asked questions, debated issues honestly, but didn't really probe into what I knew were deep divides among Americans, distances that seemed larger and more unbridgeable than the distance between me and them. My foreignness seemed to make it easier for Americans to ask me questions and try to understand my perspective, when they might have simply made judgments about their own compatriots.

I'm writing about America as I experienced it before September 11, 2001. America went mad after the 9/11 attacks, and in the process, took large parts of the world with it. But I'm talking about a simpler time, for all its own troubles.

In college, so many people commented on the fact that I spoke English so well, or asked me if I had slept on a bed growing up. Even in my privileged, small liberal arts college I chuckled at how many of my fellow students believed me when I told them that the postcard of a small mud hut with a thatched roof surrounded by the yellow brilliance of mustard flowering was, in fact, my childhood home.

Then there were the conversations where naively I tried to get some recognition of Nepal. I would ask, "Well you know about Mount Everest, right?"

And the best response I ever got: "Of course, that's the volcano that just erupted!"

"Yes," I remember replying dryly.

In college, most of my courses were outward-looking. Post-colonial literature, anthropology, middle-eastern history, even Indian dance. Looking back now, I have to wonder if I was deliberately avoiding learning about the United States. Well, there was that modern American literature class, but that was probably explained by my love of literature. It wasn't that I was avoiding America, but that in America the whole world existed and was possible. In America,

I was moved to tears reading Palestinian poetry. In America, I read Frantz Fanon and understood my world in a substantively different way. In America, I interacted with students—Americans and those from all over the globe. In America, I discovered the world in a small town in Massachusetts, and for this I will always be grateful.

This was the best part of my American experience. A place where it was possible not only to study and understand other histories and journeys, but where I met and learned from bright stars from all over the world. To me, this makes America different from any other country I've experienced. It's such a smart strategy, one that other countries should emulate as much as the American accent, slouchy jeans, and hoodies. But over time, I have realized how many American are excluded from these opportunities that shaped and guided me.

Perhaps as a result of long admiring the country from afar, I truly believed that at the foundation of this country was a belief that America is a nation of immigrants united by a set of values. That the scientists, PhD students, nurses, small business owners, laundry operators, cooks, and busboys, that all of us together, from all over the world, make America better, stronger, more resilient, and more competitive. I didn't realize how deeply I believed in this until the unthinkable happened in this country I had chosen for myself and my family.

When did we fall in love with New York? I've tried so many times to pinpoint the moment, or the week, the month, or even the year that it happened. Sometime in the last seven years, Elias and I have found home here. It's more home than not home. We have fallen in love with New York, and it's a mature love that doesn't blind us to its faults. At the core of it, I love New York because it has loved us. As corrupt as its politics are, as mind-numbing as its bureaucracy, there is no denying that New York City is a vibrant immigrant city. I smile when people call it a majority minority city. When we are the majority, then maybe we can let go of the word minority?

It's tough to say anything new or unique about New York City; it is so described in literature, in poetry, in song, and in cinema. The city pulses with energy. And yet it feels like a series of interconnected villages, each neighborhood distinct from the other, with people living incredibly local lives.

New York City's imperfections are not hidden away. There is no veil of pretense. Parts of the sub-way station ceilings can fall in front of you and you will feel lucky that they didn't land on your head. You will marvel at either the size or the number of rats scurrying on the subway tracks. The stench of the woman who doesn't have a place to shower or use the toilet is hard to ignore. Even if we rush by, we can't un-see the man lying on the sidewalk on a bitterly cold winter day.

This is also the saddest part of living in New York.

I'm online one night when I see a Facebook post for a Women's March on Washington. I quickly sign up to go. I need to do something, I need to show up for myself and for so many others. I want my daughters to know that we still have choices in how we respond, how we resist. For once, my tolerant, flexible, adaptable self cannot and will not accept.

My anger, and my refusal to accept the political environment, prompts me to seek out other like-minded people. I need in-person contact, almost as an antidote to the hours spent late at night staring at my phone screen, which is starting to feel especially unproductive. Resistance is active and communal, much of the online-only actions feel are starting to feel like isolated, individual consumption, and too passive for the feelings that are starting to simmer in me.

My friend Sarah (the same one who verified our Craigslist apartment), her daughter, Meira, Juni, and I get on a bus on the twentieth of January. I decide to leave three-year-old Maya at home with Elias. I feel relieved to be doing something, and also am relieved that we'll be on a bus during the inauguration— so we won't be watching it. Instead, we arrived in Washington, DC, and are greeted by our close friend and neighbor, Dana, who is making a film about the Women's March. She films us getting off the bus with our children, and interviews us in the nearby head-quarters of the National Women's Democratic Club, which was once the home of Eleanor Roosevelt. Dana and her crew are using part of the house as a staging and interview area. I see photos of Hillary Clinton all over the house. Young Hillary, and older Hillary. This is clearly a house that was preparing to celebrate on election night. I imagine plans being can-celed, and perhaps an inner circle of women staying up and processing the results, trying to understand what happened.

The Democratic Club is having a sign-making party, and we are welcomed to join in with our chil-dren. My sign says "We Will Resist" in big letters. Juni's sign says, "Girls Rule, You Don't." The women in the room are of all ages, though mostly white. It crosses my mind that we are in a majority black city, but no one would know this from the room we are in.

However, there are women from all over the country who have traveled to DC for the March.

A young woman starts to sing as we make our signs. She has a pure, strong, beautiful voice, and as she sings "Hallelujah," other women start to join in. I hear Juni's voice among the many voices and my eyes well up. When I look up, I see many women wiping their eyes, or just openly crying as they sing. I feel privileged to be in that room with Juni.

The next morning, our delightful hosts, Sarah's aunt and uncle, drive us into the city, as close to the starting point of the march as possible. Sarah's aunt decides to join us, and another friend has flown in from Denver to march with us. Our group of four adults and two children gets out of the car and starts walking toward the meeting location. We immediately feel buoyed by the energy of the group. There is a festive, celebratory air, a sense of defiance and humor and yes, I'll use the word sisterhood, a word I don't think I have ever actually written or spoken before. The signs are witty and smart; some of them are creative works of art. Juni and Meira are having such fun reading the signs, though I know I will get a lot of questions afterward. Some of the language is questionable for a seven-year-old audience, but I reassure myself that these are exceptional times.

We walk, we chant, and we embrace the experience. At one point we get on the Smithsonian carousel on the Washington Mall, surrounded by world-famous museums—the Museum of American History, the Museum of Natural History, and the Air and Space Museum are all around us. We balance our signs, holding them high, even as our arms ache. The crowds around us cheer us on. We move up and down on the horses, our spirits lifted by the crowds and the defiant yet loving atmosphere of the day, of so many people who have come together to express themselves and their hopes and expectations of their country. It's a scene I could never have imagined. Sitting on a merry-go-round horse with my seven-year-old daughter, carrying political signs, knowing already that we are part of an important moment in history. It is exhilarating.

Hands down, our favorite chant is "We want a leader, not a creepy Tweeter." My daughter delights in this chant, and to be honest, so do I. When I tell Juni that I will be writing about our time at the Women's March, her first question to me is if I will include the chant. Of course, sweetheart. Of course.

Juni hasn't brought the sign she made the day before. My pragmatic daughter knew she wouldn't want to carry it all day long. There is a moment when she disappears from my sight, and just as I feel the first bubbles of panic multiplying, she reappears, holding a magnificent hand-colored sign that says, "We Will Be Watching You" adorned with some large googly eyes. It is perfect. She carries it for the rest of the day.

The group around us continues to be in high spirits for the rest of the time we march. Several times, women ask our girls who they are with, and people give way as we follow them as they sometimes run ahead. For me, the most powerful thing about the gathering, apart from its sheer numbers, is the inter-generational outpouring. Dads with their daughters, grandmothers, mothers, children of all ages, including many infants. It is the biggest crowd that I have ever been part of, and I feel supported, heard, and understood by over 500,000 strangers.

"The next time we go to a protest, we'll be better prepared."

"Yeah, like our signs will be painted on both sides so people in front of us and behind us can see."

"We'll know what to expect. I mean, this is just our first march."

I smile to myself, eavesdropping on Juni and Meira's conversation. I love their assumption that there are going to more protests. Yes, we should. Yes, we will, I think to myself. I watch Juni's face for any clues as to what she is thinking about. She is hard to read sometimes, my wise (and wise-ass) child who holds her feelings deeply.

After taking part in the march, I am determined to hold onto the feelings that it inspires. I feel energized, and at the same time I am restless for action, no matter how small. I don't want to be a bystander in what feels like one of the most important political moments of my lifetime. It is certainly the most important and far-reaching political change in my life.

A few days after the march, I am glad to see an email from the organizers announcing "10 Actions in 100 Days." The first is to send Women's March postcards to our elected officials. The organizers provide a graphic template that can be downloaded and printed at home, or at a more official printer. It doesn't take me long. I check with Elias that he feels comfortable using the Buunni space for this purpose; then I post an event on the Cafe's Facebook Page to get together and write postcards.

I have no idea what the response will be, but I take a guess and order one hundred postcards to be printed (the printer gives me a discount when he hears what it is for!), buy postcard stamps, and collect all the random, spare pens lying around our apartment and head over to the cafe. I print out a list of names and addresses that someone on our local parents' email list has very helpfully shared, along with some bullet points with some sample messages for people to adapt.

I hesitate at first, about openly bringing politics to Buunni. I want Buunni to be a place that is welcoming to all, that in embracing some doesn't exclude others. But as the post-election chaos grows into something increasingly dangerous, I realize that this is not a time to be polite about politics. The stakes are too high, and it is not simply a matter of agreeing to disagree on economic policy or our theories of change. Political engagement has become a matter of protecting our families, our small businesses, and our collective American dream.

That a coffee shop should be nonpolitical is a very new notion, anyway. As I read about the history of coffeehouses, I learn that even in this county, as recently as the 1970s, coffeehouses played an important part of in mobilizing against the Vietnam War. I'm not interested in strictly partisan politics. I don't believe any one party is sacred, but rather believe in policy platforms and coherence, and in individual actions and candidates, particularly those who are not fueled and corrupted by special interests. As an immigrant-owned small business, not only is our ability to thrive and claim our home here threatened, but the notion of American stories like ours—American families like ours—are under siege. To be polite and afraid to offend seems laughable in this moment. I can welcome differences about how to get to a common goal, but now it seems the goal itself is in question.

I have decades of paperwork and rule-following and playing the role of the "good immigrant" behind me. It is clear to me now that it is not enough. It will never be enough if the current waves of xenophobia, anti-immigrant, and racist rhetoric take hold and find life and sustenance in American institutions. It is a moral moment. A moment to stand for human rights, civil rights, and liberties that are too hard-won to give up without a fight. No, this is not a time for political politeness.

I'm fidgeting with the postcards and pens and waiting nervously for the first people to show up. I have snacks and drinks laid out on the communal table. A few people start arriving. Some of them are our regular customers, other faces are new to me and I'm curious about how they found out about the event. Some say a friend forwarded them the information; an older woman, who makes a point of telling me she's not on Facebook, tells me someone printed and posted the announcement in her building's elevator. I go over the materials we have, and people start writing. As we write, we talk about issues that matter to us, about our fears and what has motivated us to do this. I'm struck that in addition to writing about opposition to things, people are also writing notes of thanks to elected representatives that are doing a good job in representing their constituents. I look up and see that our tiny space is full. My order of one hundred post-cards is gone in the first hour.

We are not naive—a few postcards do not a resistance make—but sitting together and writing, talking through the issues in person, sharing information about upcoming events, actions, and opportunities, is not only essentially therapeutic because it allows us to express our feelings, but it reminds us that we are not alone, that we are many, that we feel strongest when we are taking action rather than fretting at home, alone, staring at our screens. The times require us to be part of a bigger family and a community of conversation. We gather, we meet, we talk, and we write. These gatherings at Buunni become something that sustains us. My next order is for a thousand postcards.

Half a block away, at the local public school where Juni studies, school kids are also talking. Here is a grownup, this guy who wanted to be president, who is now president—President Meanie—who behaves in ways that would take any of them straight to the principal's office.

I am clearing up the perpetual mess in our living room one Saturday and I hear my youngest, Maya, who is three, sing-song rhyming:

Donald Trump, takes a dump,
And he drops an orange lump.

Like everyone in New York City, sometimes I need a coffee shop to work in. On mornings when I work at Buunni, I love being in the space. To borrow from Melody, I receive the hug that the warmth of the space emanates. I work, and greet people, and listen in on conversations. The art on the walls elicited many reactions this morning. People laugh, comment, take pictures. A mother and daughter walk in. I know they have been to the cafe many times. This morning, however, they sit at the narrow counter where the Resistance Box is placed. The daughter is delighted. "Wow. Look at this! This box, with postcards, pens, and stamps. This is amazing." "Tiny spaces with a big impact," Melody said. "Small spaces, big ideas."

I think, Small spaces, big heart.

I scan the email I've just opened with growing interest. Nina Turner, the president of Our Revolution, a group formed to take forward the energy that was unleashed during the Bernie Sanders campaign, is going to be speaking at the Riverside Church. I check my calendar, and it is on a rare day that I can attend. I instantly think of my dad. He'd want to go too. I get tickets, and the next day my father and I are outside the massive Riverside Church waiting for the doors to open.

There are mostly women of all ages, from their twenties to some who appear to be well over seventy. Eventually the crowd includes more young men, but they are not the majority. Like most parts of New York City, the participants are multi-hued and multi-generational.

People mill about on the steps. My dad and I chat intermittently. In that peculiar limbo of waiting, our conversation is halting. Finally the doors open and we get seats near the front. It's a large space, and it's about a third full. My dad recalls that this is in this very Riverside Church where Martin Luther King delivered his famous "Beyond Vietnam" speech, a speech that was criticized at the time by both the

Washington Post and the *New York Times*, but reverberated throughout the world for its courage in linking the US civil rights movement with the international peace movement.

Today, the starting speakers are hesitant. They seem unused to public speaking, but they are earnest and good natured. There are local candidates running through the Green Party, representatives of local independent news outlets, local-level organizers emphasizing how local politics most shape our lives while we are focused on the national political dramas. A young woman from Connecticut fills the room with a shot of energy, and an African American youth leader speaks with passion and eloquence about the Movement for Black Lives. He speaks with a respect and dignity that intrigues me. Finally, Nina Turner is introduced by a young man named Jabari Brisport. He exudes the charm of a local boy, Brooklyn born and bred, and he's re-branding socialism. "Try socialism," he says with a smile and a bit of mischief. His charisma is evident, and my dad comments, "This young man will go far in politics. Listen to him speak."

Nina Turner is magic. She draws us in, she expresses herself with an easy fluency, and her stories are fueled by passionate persuasiveness. And heart. She weaves the deeply personal with the deeply political. She talks about her grandmother, and tells the story of the three bones—the wishbone, the jawbone, and the backbone—as being essential to success in life.

The wishbone represents our hopes and dreams, what motivates and drives us. A strong jawbone enables us to speak truth to power, and to make our voice count. And a solid backbone gives us the courage to endure difficulties and tough times.

It has been a long, long time since I've been so moved by a speaker. Moved to laugh and to cry. I see my dad's eyes well up too. We go home deeply affected. I think about it for days.

I am in the room when Hillary Clinton says she's joining the resistance. My heart sinks a little.

I have been invited by a colleague to the fundraising luncheon for a women's organization. Hillary Clinton is speaking publicly for the first time since the election, and the discussion is being moderated by Christiane Amanpour. After a spirited and warm conversation, Clinton says that she is now a private citizen and a member of the resistance. Coming from someone who has been a presidential candidate, the secretary of state, a senator from New York, and the first lady, I find the statement a little disingenuous. One thing I know: to be powerful and meaningful, the movement must be fueled and led by everyday people—political outsiders, and not insiders.

The "Resistance" brand is being corporatized and monetized. Resistance merchandise, branding, events, books, and speakers—all are trying to make a buck out of the newfound political activism of people who have been, politically-speaking, asleep at the wheel. Sometimes I worry that Buunni's social activism will be perceived in this way too, as either trying to curry favor with our community or as a blurring of selling coffee and selling the resistance vibe.

Coffeehouses, too, have been corporatized and neutralized. In place of revolutionary ideas and political organizing, the modern coffeehouse is depoliticized and a pleasant but transactional place. Where people go to work as individuals, inured to others, protected by headphones and the empty glare of the screens in front of them. The independent coffeehouse culture rebels against this notion, by drawing on an older and more interesting tradition and history.

I'm going through Buunni's social media accounts, as I do every day, when I see something that excites me: a coffee-related media account that I follow has announced a nation-wide coffee fundraiser for the ACLU, the American Civil Liberties Union. This is in response to a weekend of protests. Immigration lawyers have been scrambling to challenge an Executive Order, the Muslim Ban, which prohibits refugees and immigrants from a long list of countries from entering the US. I sign Buunni up for the effort. We will match and double customer donations up to $500. Sprudge.com makes a map of coffee shops that sign up for this initiative. Support pours from coffeehouses all over the country, and I am proud that Buunni is part of this collective effort. At Buunni, we raised close to $1500. I later find out that over eight hundred independent coffee shops across the country joined.

Think about that! Eight hundred coffee shops, representing every state in the country, have overwhelmed Sprudge's small staff; they are barely able to keep up. They hoped to raise $100,000 and ended up raising close to $500,000. In one weekend. I am awed by our collective power, many small independent coffee shops coming together to stand with people, to stand for a welcoming community. I am proud to be a part of it.

All coffee-shop owners and workers know that it's about so much more than the coffee. What keeps people coming back are the relationships, the human connections, and a place to go that is not home and not work. We are built around the idea of people coming together, of being a welcoming space. Our ability to raise money quickly is impressive, for sure, but our real power could be in the hundreds, perhaps even thousands, of coffeehouses hosting locally relevant community conversations, talking things out in person, taking a stand for the kind of country we want for ourselves and for our children. What about registering people to vote? What about getting people engaged, interested, heck, even excited about politics?

Coffeehouses have historically been places of learning; of making business deals; scientific, literary, political, philosophical, and economic discussions; and political revolutions. Art, performance and satire, great ideas, creative solutions, and political movements are born in coffeehouses. I want to find out more. I am pulled to reclaim this great past tradition and to find a way to apply to it our present moment.

Shadows

On an unseasonably warm February morning, Elias, Juni, Maya, and I head to midtown on the A train. We are going to a rally in Times Square in support of Muslims—to be in solidarity. Before we go, I try to prepare Juni and explain to her why we are choosing this fantastically beautiful day to go to crowded Times Square instead of our splendid local Fort Tryon Park, or at least the three playgrounds in walking distance from our house where Juni and Maya have run and squealed and tumbled endlessly for a large part of their short existence on this planet.

I'm not sure what to say, so I start with a playground scenario. I ask her, if someone is being mean to one of her friends in the playground, will she stick up for her friend? She nods yes. I say, "Well, Donald Trump is being mean to Muslims. We're going to the rally to stick up for them."

Then I realize she might not understand what Muslims are! She knows about Jews because she went to the Jewish Y nursery in our neighborhood (and would occasionally come home singing Shabbat Shalom), and I think she knows about Christians and Hindus (the faiths her parents have been raised in), but Muslim? So I say: "Junmun, there are billions of Muslims in the world, in Asia, Africa, the Middle East, here in the US. Remember you played with Imran in Ethiopia? He's Muslim. His mom, Kume, is Muslim. Your beloved Rama is Muslim, too." She lights up at the names of people she knows and loves.

We take the subway to Times Square, and Maya already has that slightly dazed, half-crazed look that she gets when she's sleepy. She smiles gorgeous, huge smiles at strangers, rolls her head around, giggles and wiggles—all signs, believe it or not, that she will imminently fall asleep. We get out of the subway and walk to the starting point of the rally at 48th and Broadway, zigzagging though the crowds with Maya in the stroller and me clutching at a skipping Juni's hand. By the time we start seeing people holding signs and hear the blare of the bad sound system, Maya is fast asleep in the stroller. A few minutes later, Juni, who is a great reader, starts asking me questions that would be hard to answer in the quiet of our living room. They are near impossible to tackle in this crowded and loud atmosphere.

"Mama, what is democracy?"

"Baby, it's a long explanation, I'll tell you when we go home, okay?"

"Okay."

"Mama, what does KKK mean?"

"Juni, we'll talk about it when we get home, okay?"

"Okay."

"Mama, what does fascism mean?"

This one is right after a group around us starts chanting, "No Trump, No KKK, No fascism in the USA"

"Juni, we'll talk about all of this at home. It's hard to explain here, in the crowd and the noise."

"Okay . . . can we go to Chocolate World? Even just to look around?"

"Yes, baby, we can do that," I answer with relief.

"What do you miss?"

The question sucks the air out of my lungs. I can't breathe. An eternity of seconds passes in silence. I am transported to another time and place. I'm running up the concrete stairs to a flat cement roof warm under my bare feet, giggling with my cousins, racing them and the monsoon clouds so we'll be lying down on our backs before the first drops fall. The heat of the sun, absorbed by the concrete, warms our backs, while the first fat droplets of rain bounce off our faces. The drops that fall on the roof create a steam, and then, as the rain falls in earnest, a welcome cool. I can smell the first drops of rain on the cement roof. I am conscious that I am blinking rapidly, and that the silence has gone beyond politeness.

"Um . . . lots of things. Some things are hard to explain."

I'm troubled by his question. By the enormity of it. It threatens to unmoor me. Of course there are the easy answers: I miss friends and relatives and language and food. But I also miss what no longer exists. The rice paddies behind my childhood home have been taken over by Nepalis' collective dream of a house in Kathmandu, no matter where, how tiny, what shape or height. This hunger has devoured the rice paddies and fertile soil that once circled the city in a garland of small farms and providing the city their bounty. I miss eating spiced grapefruit on the roof, and basking in the winter sun. Except my cousin Srijana, who is fair-skinned and so pretty. She remains in the shade, but even she can't resist and slips her bare feet out into the sun—her toes, the only part of her that she will allow to tan. I miss the smell of the dry winter air, the ease of belonging somewhere, and not having to defend or explain how I got there. I never had to express gratitude to my old country the way my new home country repeatedly demands.

I smile at the man in front of me.

"I miss everything."

I witness this same unspoken unraveling recently in a Nigerian man. Elias and I are at an event hosted by the Business Center for New Americans. Successful refugee and immigrant entrepreneurs who have received financing from the center to expand their businesses are being honored. As part of the program, there is a panel discussion. A young, thin, black man on the stage talks about how he learned about food preparation at one of New York's well-known food establishments and grew to become a chef there. After a number of years, he left this good job to start out on his own. Now he's grown his food and catering business from humble beginnings, from selling meals from the trunk of his car outside the Nigerian community churches. When families came out of church after the service, they would pick up food infused with flavors that took them back to their childhoods. He now co-owns a food truck and catering business.

He's a lively speaker, and during the Q&A session, he entertains the audience with his stories. Then an older white American gentleman asks, "You've done so well here, but I'm sure you had to give up a lot too. What do you miss from your home country?"

The young man on the stage takes a deep breath and goes quiet. The thud, thud, thud of my heartbeat is pulsing in my ears. I can't take my eyes off him. I know that while he stands there, frozen, his mind is racing, a thousand miles away.

"I miss nothing. Why should I miss anything? I miss nothing," he's almost shouting.

As Buunni grows, we start to have a few wholesale clients. If Elias and I had more time, or were able to hire someone to help us with this, I think our wholesale accounts could grow significantly. For now, we are simply thankful for those who find us and ask us to supply their restaurants and cafés with our coffee. One of these is Injera, an Ethiopian restaurant in Greenwich Village that found us through word of mouth. It's a husband and wife team; the wife, Roman, is from Ethiopia, and the husband, Pierre, is French. Their food is delicious, and it's one of those small New York City spaces, like our own, where they do a lot with a little bit of space.

One day, Elias receives an urgent order from Pierre. When he gets there, he cannot find Pierre. But one of the staff, Julio, is there to receive the order. As he's handing over the coffee to Julio, Elias says, "Wow, these smells remind me of home. It smells so good in here. Is that also enjera I smell?"

The traditional soft Ethiopian staple bread is an item that, even in Addis Ababa, many families buy rather than baking at home. Elias wonders who the chef is in the kitchen. Maybe one of Roman's relatives?

"Thanks, man, yeah, I'm getting the enjera ready before our dinner crowd."

"You make the enjera?"

"Yeah. Sure I do. Roman's mom taught me. I cook all the food."

Elias is dumbfounded. A Mexican guy called Julio is cooking food from Ethiopia and the smells are bringing him home to his childhood.

"Wow. That's impressive. I'm rushing now, but I'm definitely coming back to try it soon, okay?"

That night as he's finishing telling me this story, Elias concludes, "Mexicans do everything in America. What would happen to this country without them? In America, Julio even makes the enjera."

We have been approached from the early days of Buunni about expanding our business. Each time, it's an exciting prospect, but with Maya still a baby and Juni just starting school, juggling our family life with my work with its frequent travels and a growing business is already daunting as it is. Elias manages the coffee operations and most of our family logistics. We make a conscious decision to focus on nourishing our three babies—our two daughters and our Buunni.

Juni and Maya are delightful children. Warm and generous and social. I am the huggiest and cuddliest of Mamas. I am love itself and the source of emotional nourishment. But I hate myself when I lose my temper and see the startled and hurt look in Juni's eyes, moments before her eyes brighten and then well up with tears, the quiver of her lips just after I slam my hand down on the table. No one talks about this. The anger, no, the rage, of being a mother. As much as I love the hugs and cuddles, as much as I am the soft Mama, I wouldn't be honest without writing about the other truths of motherhood. I am surprised at how loud my own voice can get when the anger rises in me and I honest-to-god yell at my kids. Being a mother is the hardest thing I've ever done. The best, most beautiful, loveliest, loneliest, darkest, hardest, most strenuous thing I have ever done in my life. I often joke that being a CEO of a global non-profit, my professional role, is easy compared to mother-hood. Going to work often feels like an escape. My cousin jokes that she started drinking whiskey after she had her two boys.

All this, even though I have a partner in the true sense of the word in Elias. He does far more than his "share," and still I struggle. I'm good at the hugs and kisses, reading to them, talking with them, but the daily routines, the cajoling, the negotiating, the nit-picking, the arguing, feel like more than I can bear some days.

By the time our girls are both in the same school, I know Elias is itching to grow Buunni. And we have already signed up to be one of the local small busi-nesses in the newly renovated George Washington Bridge Bus Terminal about ten blocks from our cur-rent location. But years have passed, and the bus ter-minal renovation is hopelessly off-track and the delays are the subject of local news pieces and community hearings. There's no guarantee when this project might take off. Luckily for us, we've only had to pay a deposit with a lease, but it's hard to plan anything else when we don't know when the bus terminal project might pick up pace.

When we travel around the city, I see how closely Elias looks at empty storefronts, assessing how far they are from a bus stop, or wondering out loud how far away the nearest independent coffeeshop might be. We both know that we've rooted and grown Buunni in our own neighborhood, and we're eager to try our hand at another location. We decide on Riverdale, a neighborhood about a ten-minute drive from us, where quite a few of our friends and neighbors have started to move. It's the New York City rotation— as rents and apartment prices increase in other neighborhoods, many people have moved into our neighborhood, and now our rents are going up and those looking for better value, an extra bedroom or just a bit more space, have started to look elsewhere.

Part of our decision is practical. We want a location Elias will be able to manage while remaining grounded in our own neighborhood, where our girls are in school, and where our home and business life are centered.

I feel a pain in my chest and then a deep anger spreads through my body. I'm reading a headline that causes this physical reaction. Parents in a hospital, waiting while their infant is in surgery, are arrested and taken away by ICE agents.

The objective, professional part of my brain thinks about the implications, how much needless suffering, pain, and death will be caused because people will now rightly be afraid of seeking medical attention. From a public health perspective, this is a disaster.

But I'm a mama. And the anger inside me is for what these parents are experiencing. Last night, Maya, now almost four years old, was up with a hacking cough. I was so worried. I tried to soothe her as best I could—it was paramount to be close, to be watching and caring for her. She wasn't in any danger, she just wasn't feeling well and was uncomfortable. And I felt so helpless, even though I was right there next to her. I imagine someone taking me away from her and must quickly push the unbearable thought away. What I can't even bear to think about, so many mothers are experiencing in their encounters with the US Government.

I know in my heart that this would have never been done to a white family. Is this what America has always been for brown and black people? This is a country of such extremes. Such beauty and talent and skill, and so few people who are afforded the right to enjoy them. Not everyone needs to read the books I've been lucky enough to read, but everyone has the right to understand their own history, to be moved by art, to keep learning, to grow, to stumble upon deeper truths, to stand in someone else's shoes. Yet it seems America has created a segregation so deep that not only is it not clear how to build bridges, but something as crude as creating a physical wall has become a rallying cry.

The chasm between the possibility of America and the reality of the country which is now mine has never seemed wider. While so much of our attention is on Donald Trump —amplifying his agenda or resisting it—he is merely the symptom of a disease that is eating this country up from the inside. The roots of the disease are deep and seemingly unchangeable and reside in millions of hearts and minds—a country built on theft, looting, rape, and war, unacknowledged and unatoned for. This history cannot rest in the past, so it now consumes our present. And it will steal our future too unless we can deal with it, no matter how ugly it may be, and how much pain we might feel.

Buunni Riverdale, our second location, is stuck. We've made the classic mistake of falling in love with a space and ignoring and waving away all the signals we should have been paying close attention to. Unlike our first coffee shop, we've never met the landlord for our second location in Riverdale, in the Bronx, only with the representative of the management company. He is gruff and borderline rude during our first meeting. His tone is so off-putting that in hindsight we should have reconsidered right there. But we love the sunny two-level space on Riverdale Avenue alongside a string of restaurants and bars. To us, what is missing on that strip is a place like Buunni. A place for excellent coffee, and a place to hang out, meet friends, or read a book. We know many people from our neighborhood have been moving to Riverdale in the never-ending New York City quest for more affordable housing.

Growing a small business like ours in a city as expensive and bureaucratic as New York City is not for the faint of heart. We are many months delayed, and our nerves are being tested. Is our success at Buunni in Washington Heights just a case of beginner's luck? Have we bitten off more than we can chew?

At one point, I confide in my mom about how worried I am. She contacts her astrologer in Kathmandu via Facebook messenger, and tells me that the stars are against us for another few months. "Nani," as she calls me affectionately, "don't worry, I will ask them to do a puja. And let me go to the space and light some incense. Don't worry. It will get better."

I figure incense and prayers can't hurt. We'll take anything we can.

I'm on the phone with our architect, talking to him about the delays in permits and approvals. "We are losing every day." I feel the tightness in my throat, and my voice sounds strange, like it's coming from far away. I try desperately to hold it together, but my eyes sting. *Oh god, don't let me cry on the phone with this guy.* "We are stretched to a breaking point. I don't know what else I can say to you. Please."

The unacceptably long delays in opening our Riverdale location are somehow no one's fault. These are the moments when I think we are insane for taking on the level of risk we have. All our money, apart from what I'm putting into my retirement fund, is going into growing the business. The first time around, I took a loan from the retirement fund and maxed out all the credit cards in a well-sequenced operation. This time the retirement plan and personal credit cards are off-limits. You might call that progress. But the delay is a double whammy. We are losing time and paying rent, in addition to losing income we could have been making if the space were open. It is crazy-making, and particularly so because no one takes any responsibility or seems to be in any hurry. Our position feels precarious once again.

There is no doubt Elias and I are taking on more than what is "advisable." But part of the fun and thrill of being an entrepreneur is that for all the advice you get, you can still do what you want. You can still do what excites you, and what feels right in your gut. Almost always, that is not what the experts advise.

For all our plans and ideas, our major constraint is capital. We don't want investors outside of a few friends and family. We know we don't want to give up our independence, and accepting large outside investment will change what we value most about owning our own business. This results in a patchwork of funding from trusted friends and family, which sometimes feels like we're putting a series of mini-band-aids on a large gash.

Then, just when we need it most, we find out that we're approved for a small business loan through our local bank. This is truly a gift. I could cry—I do cry. Happy tears, as Juni calls them. The loan is backed by the Small Business Administration. This is a milestone for a small, family-owned micro-business. The six-figure loan makes us feel like we're in the big leagues now. A bank has decided to loan us money. That is pretty neat.

We sign the papers at our local bank branch across the street from our apartment. This is the same bank we had gone to seven years ago, excited to open our first business accounts. Elizabeth, our favorite banker there, herself an immigrant from Nigeria, helps us with the paperwork. After we sign the papers, we cross the street and head straight to our local Mexican restaurant. We order two margaritas. It is eleven in the morning. We are celebrating. We feel official.

Elias is always in motion, in a state of doing. His long arms and legs working, fixing, walking, cleaning, cooking, chopping, caring, repairing. Often humming or listening to music. On lazy Sunday mornings in Addis Ababa, I tease him about reading the newspaper, listening to music, and watching TV at the same time. Maybe each is too still for him, but combined, they make a perfect recipe for his unique style of relaxation.

When we drove around the neighborhood in Addis Ababa where he had lived his whole life, I joked that he should just keep one hand outside his window to make it easier to wave to everyone as he passes by. It would be more efficient that way, since he was constantly greeting everyone. Once, when we were shopping for vegetables at an open-air market, an elderly woman struggled to get up from where she was sitting behind her mounds of neatly stacked onions, tomatoes, and large green *qarya* hot peppers and came to us with such determination, I worried that we had done something wrong and offended her. Instead, she hugged Elias hard and asked him to lower his head so she could kiss him on both cheeks. She remembered how mischievous he was as a child and scolded him then for not remembering her.

When I first introduced him to my Egyptian friend Sarah over dinner and wine, she tearily announced, "You look like my ancestors!" His skin, always warm, is dark bronze, and his face with his almond eyes and high cheekbones evokes ancient Egypt.

Elias excels in understatement, and you would be forgiven for thinking him distant or aloof. His looks are what created the cliché of tall, dark, and handsome. As handsome as he is, it's his interior landscape that fascinates me. He carries a lot under the surface. Even now, I feel a childish delight when I elicit an uncontrollable giggle from him, or when he details a blow-by-blow description of events. These are rewards for those who have known him a long time.

Elias is a quiet guy. Except when he's talkative. Sometimes, occasionally, he starts talking about something and gets really animated. His gestures, his laugh, his body—all telling the story along with his words. These are special occasions, and I go quiet and listen, forbidding anything to interrupt these moments. He could be talking about anything. It could be something that happened at the Café, or something on the news.

Over the time I've known him, the vertical lines that form when his brow is furrowed in concentration have deepened. The silver in his hair, at first barely noticeable, is now apparent at first glance. Very soon the balance will shift in his curly hair and the silver will win over the black. The gap between his two front teeth is prized in his home country, but this special trait is not understood here in America. It is part of the vastness that cannot be translated. That gap in his teeth remains, though the teeth are whiter than they were, a result of the specifically American preoccupation with six-month dental visits and teeth-whitening regimens.

Elias has adjusted remarkably well to our life in New York. I often think this comes from him being so comfortable in his own skin. He has a confidence that is understated, but palpable. I admire his ability to learn, change, and adapt, while remaining utterly himself. He has whiter teeth, his speech and his emails are peppered with Americanisms, but he is at his core the same man I fell in love with and married in Addis Ababa. And now, just like before, I joke that everyone seems to know him now here too. He greets everyone in our Washington Heights neighborhood.

Elias and I steal moments together when we can. I get truly grumpy when I don't have enough time with him. I crave time to talk, to laugh, to sit close and breathe the same air with my husband. It is remarkable how spending time together can renew and rejuvenate us, reunite us, remind us of our common purpose, our priorities and our life goals, and just lighten our mood. I am still greedy for time with him. Sometimes I remind our children that before they came along, I had their Papa all to myself.

The George Washington Bus Terminal renovations are finally done, and we're told to start construction in our space. But the numbers tell us that our bank loan covers us for only one location out of the two we have under way, and the contractor's estimate on our bus terminal location has doubled during the years that have passed waiting for the private developers and the Port Authority to complete the renovations. We are running out of friends and family to approach. We very well might be going back into the retirement fund and the personal credit cards.

Why not take it slower and wait? This doesn't feel like an option. After all, we did slow down during the first four years of Buunni, knowing our girls needed us, and with my working full-time in a senior role. Elias had significant parenting responsibilities, and supported me with my crazy schedule and travel, but now that both our daughters are going to the local public school, Elias is itching to grow the business. We are both forty-four years old. It feels like now or never. Never doesn't feel like much of an option, so it has to be now.

And then springs forth the latest opportunity: a possible fourth location. A coffee shop that opened just before we first opened Buunni, in the neighborhood just north of us, wants to sell. Like us, it's a business owned by a couple with small children. They are tired of the grinding realities of running a coffee shop, and in their case, a bakery as well, and they want to exit from the business. They want to move on, to spend more time with their kids and go back to the professional roles they had given up to start their business. Elias and I can't believe our luck. In fact, we feel honored to be in conversations to buy it. We know how hard Nick and Nichole have worked to build their business, and we will do everything we can to continue what they started, and to build on it. We've been deliberately avoiding the Inwood neighborhood where their shop is located because we didn't want to compete directly with another independent coffeehouse. Now that they are looking for an exit plan, we see a wonderful opportunity to continue to serve the community if we can make the numbers work.

There are also exciting possibilities of partnering with other local small businesses and community organizations. We have a good feeling about these opportunities, and are ready to do the work to bring them to fruition. The one thing that is non-negotiable for us is maintaining our independence. We are fiercely protective of Buunni, our labor of love. We like the choices that we make—such as choosing compostable cups, which are more expensive, and hosting free community events that mean that we are not always maximizing profits. We want a healthy, thriving business that supports us, but that also makes a positive contribution to our staff and to our community. If the business isn't good for people and for the community, then what is it for?

One step at a time, I keep telling myself. Don't get ahead of yourself.

We are in an ugly and painful national moment, a time of outing some big truths. Men respected and admired by society have been sexually harassing women with impunity, this I think we've all known for a long time. But the scale, and the repeated patterns, have shocked even those who have experienced sexual harassment and inappropriate sexual conduct—how pervasive it is, and how power has wielded silence, and how complicit we have all been.

As I read about new allegations, and the seriously creepy patterns of multiple women with the same story coming out publicly, I have a tight ball in the pit of my stomach. That's where I've kept my self-blame and shame. Even now, writing this, I tell myself that I didn't have it as bad as others. My story, my stories, are unexceptional. I've told myself that I am one of the lucky ones. But alongside that self-effacing (self-erasing?) narrative is a deep, simmering anger. I tell my younger self: it wasn't your fault. It was never your fault.

This moment reminds me of another. At the time, I felt I was in another world, but now, I know that these worlds and this pain are interconnected. It was 2009, and my colleague Mane and I were in Arba

Minch in Southern Ethiopia. Outwardly, this was a work trip to a city that I was fond of. A place where I had a favorite restaurant, a favorite breakfast café with a juice bar that serves heavenly freshly-squeezed, thick mango juice with a little wedge of lime. In my internal world, my thoughts were clamoring; I had found out, a few weeks before leaving for the trip, that I was pregnant. It was my first ever pregnancy. Happily, I had been successful in my many years of avoiding this exact scenario, but the last year I had spent trying to get pregnant. I was delighted and nervous and self-absorbed in the way I now realize one can only be the first time around.

We were staying in a new hotel, and at breakfast, my colleague knew to order a macchiato for me before breakfast arrived. This was unusual enough in Ethiopia (where most people drink their coffee after breakfast) that ordering coffee first needed to be followed up by a reminder, and a reassurance, that yes, in fact, you did want your coffee before breakfast, and that you would order another one after breakfast too.

Mane and I were going over the schedule of our day when my macchiato arrived. It was perfect, not too dark, not too milky, it was served in a clear four-ounce glass that showed off its layers. It was a beauty. Then I realized that not only did I have no interest in drinking it, but the fact that it was sitting on the table in front of me was making me feel nauseous. Oh boy.

While Mane continued to talk about our meetings with the female water-engineering students at Arba Minch University, my mind raced to think up a possible explanation for why I would need to leave my macchiato untouched. Anyone who knew me well would not buy an "I just don't feel like drinking it" explanation. I was a macchiato fanatic, a dedicated connoisseur. I could talk to you for hours about my favorite places in Addis Ababa to drink macchiato, and explain to you why, carefully detailing the pros and cons of ordering a macchiato in each of the above-mentioned places.

Not only that; the Ethiopian macchiato is made with steamed milk and a small amount of sugar that helps to separate the layers of espresso and milk, and therefore is different from the Italian macchiato. This drink has an oversized sentimental place in my heart. This is the drink over which Elias and I got to know each other. We talked, and met, repeatedly, over endless, countless cups of Ethiopian macchiato. In our early days, when I was too shy to say, "Hey, do you want to hang out? Shall we spend some time together?" I would simply say, "Macchiato enteta?" (Shall we have macchiato?) "Eishi," was his consistent reply. After dinner, when it was time for me to go home, Elias would ask me, "Macchiato tejialesh?" (Do you want a macchiato?) And "Eishi" would be my consistent reply.

I fell in love over many cups of macchiato, and therefore, by association, loved the drink itself. And now it sat getting cold on the table in front of me while I tried not to gag. This was to be the first of my many surprising symptoms of pregnancy. In what I took as a result of my good karma, a fly circled the drink, precariously perched on the rim of the glass, and fell in. I breathed a sigh of relief and signaled the waitress to ask her to take the drink away. Then I thought to myself, I'm not sure this is how karma really works.

Later that day, we were on campus at the Arba Minch University. My work on water had made it clear that while at a household level the responsibility for collecting and managing water was considered a woman's responsibility, when it came to professional roles, the field was almost exclusively male. My workplace, WaterAid, was often used as the example of where women in the water sector could be found. And even in our office, we didn't have any female water engineers. So I was there with Mane to hear from young women students about why so many of them were struggling and dropping out, even though many more women were enrolling in the program.

We were gathered in a large, bare room. The streams of light coming in from several small windows created patterns of light and shadow. We made a circle, several rows deep, moving our chairs—the school-type chairs that have a small writing area attached—until we had determined that everyone could hear and see. Mane introduced us. While my colloquial Amharic was pretty good, she would translate and take notes and facilitate the meeting. We'd asked to talk to the students alone, without academic faculty or university administration.

I knew the beginning of the conversation would be a warming up, a gauging of interests, and all the while they would be deciding how much to disclose, how honest to be with us, two women they had never met before. The most outspoken and confident students spoke first. They talked about being ill-prepared for the classes they were taking. Many had come from under-resourced, rural schools, where they didn't learn everything that was expected, according to the Ethiopian national high school curriculum.

A girl in a long skirt, which was clean, but very worn, raised her hand. Mane and I both nodded at her in encouragement.

"It's difficult because though we don't have to pay for classes, we don't have money for anything else. It's hard to concentrate when we have to worry about money so much. Or if we have to miss classes because we don't have certain essentials that you need as a woman."

"How many days do you miss class?"

"If I don't have supplies, I might miss four or five

days in a month. It's not just that, other basics, like detergent to wash our clothes, or soap to keep ourselves clean."

I wasn't surprised by this. I had spoken with many adolescent girls about how difficult it was for them to attend classes when they had their period. Sometimes it's the lack of sanitary pads, other times it's the lack of privacy and a place to change.

Another young woman raised her hand.

"It's really difficult it is to catch up if you've fallen behind. If you've missed classes, it's almost impossible to catch up. We try to help each other, share notes, review together, but it's not enough. And then it just confirms that as women we are not good enough. The guys and the teachers are not surprised. 'Why are you studying engineering, anyway? It's too hard, you should switch,' they say."

Another hand shot up.

"The thing is, even the ones who are supposed to be helping us, who are supposedly helping us, have their own reasons."

I couldn't see the woman who had just spoken, but her voice was strong, and I could see the others looking around and giving her a meaningful look. The dynamics in the room had just changed, and I didn't know why. There was an energy in the room, and almost on cue, I could hear rumblings of thunder outside, and then a flash of lightening.

"Tell us more, what do you mean, they have their own reasons? Surely your teachers want to help you succeed?" Mane asked.

A young woman in a traditional hairdo, her hair braided back half-way along her scalp, half snorted, "Well I don't think we need to tell you how men are. If we need help with our studies, or if we need supplies, we can get the help, but it's not free."

I started to understand what was being said. I whispered to Mane, "Ask them if they've reported the teacher."

She did, and the reply still rings in my head. "How many teachers should we report? And who exactly would we report them to?"

Now the rain was coming down. It was torrential. And we were in a dark room with gusts of wind coming in through the window. The rain was tapping out crazy rhythms on the tin roof. I have always loved the sound of rain on a tin roof. The sound reminds me of my childhood and adolescence in Nepal, of trekking in the mountains and taking shelter from the hard rain, of finding it hard to hear each other over the noisy din of the raindrops falling like pebbles on the tin roof. Now the sound reminds me of Arba Minch and these women's stories.

The academic staff was almost entirely male, and many of them recent graduates, themselves only a few years older than the students they were meant to teach. The administrative staff with any power or authority was likely almost entirely male. These students, many of them hours or days away from home for the first time, with no network, family, or friends nearby, and many in severe financial distress, were the perfect prey for these men. I'm sure many of the men would not think of themselves as predators. They might have thought they were having some form of a consensual relationship. But the power relationship was so utterly imbalanced, and one side had everything to lose or gain. Sexual harassment, sexual assault, and rape were rampant on this campus. And the people in charge of the university were the perpetrators.

As so many have noted, sexual abuse is not about sex, but about power. And sexual abuse was the biggest problem these women were facing. They were dropping out to escape the academic dreams that had become their nightmares.

Now Elias and I have two daughters. I know now that the stereotyping and rigid gender roles that I was so angry about in Nepal and Ethiopia are alive and well in the United States. It starts early here too, a pink and blue divide between infant boys and girls, and we now understand that we ourselves have much to learn about gender beyond the binary. In New York, I've felt the same anger I felt in Addis Ababa listening to my mother-in-law envision a future coffee-making Juni— at birthday parties where there are "boys tables," on playdates divided by dolls and trucks, the day when our younger daughter came home from school saying, "I don't want to wear pants, Mama, girls wear skirts and dresses."

This year, during the confirmation of a Supreme Court Judge, I hear echoes of public spectacles of the past as women are labeled "hysterical" for insisting that they be heard. I see old men discount and laugh at women of all ages when they assert that their experiences matter, that their stories are at least as valid as the ones that men have told and controlled for so long.

As it turns out, in America too, girls make the coffee.

Coffeehouse

Resistance

I'M SITTING AT BUUNNI WITH MELODY, who is a regular customer.

"I'm thinking we should close for a day this summer so we can take our full team to the beach," I say.

"That's a great idea."

"Well, we don't often get to spend time all together. Because of the shifts, someone's coming, someone's going. It's even tough to schedule a staff meeting."

"Maybe you don't have to close the café, though."

"What do you mean?"

"Well, maybe some of us regulars can watch the shop for you."

"You would do that?"

"Yes, babysitting Buunni!" she sounds delighted. "I think people would like it. It could be fun. Who doesn't want to work in a coffee shop? We can pretend for a day."

"I have to talk to Elias. I love this idea, but he might not."

Melody pauses, and gives me a long meaningful look, before she smiles. "Why do I have a feeling you will convince him?"

I'm so excited. It could be a case study in radical trust. Buunni is our baby, and yet, I'm willing to leave it with . . . not strangers. That's why it feels okay.

"Elias, we've known most of these people for six years. Some of our regulars became regulars during our first week."

I know my husband is on the verge of saying yes. And he does. And so the planning begins in earnest.

"Melody, this is America, so we have to think about liability. Everyone must sign something stating they have voluntarily signed up for this, and they assume the risks."

"Yeah, that's a good idea."

I set up a Google doc sign-up sheet for one- and two-hour volunteer shifts, and I have more responses than I know what to do with. For some shifts we assign four people when we only need two. I feel bad turning anyone away.

Before our big day, I reach out to a local journalist because I think it might be a neat local story. She writes a piece that runs the day before our trip. On the morning of our beach outing, we agree to finish the morning set up, hand over the place to our customers, and all squeeze into our minivan for our escape.

As we we're setting up, a formally dressed woman in full makeup walks in. I feel like I'm supposed to know her, but I have no idea who she is. I greet her, and she introduces herself as Cindy Hsu from CBS news. She wants to interview us; she has heard about our customer take-over.

"And, we were thinking we might follow you to the beach."

An interview is okay, but follow us to the beach? On our precious beach day? I try not to look annoyed. "We're actually really looking forward to our beach time. We'll do the interview here, but I'm not sure about you guys coming to the beach."

"Oh, we won't take long. It's just that it's television, it's very visual. We need the footage of the beach to make the story work."

I think about it for a moment. We do a quick interview, Cindy's crew films inside the café, and we exchange cell numbers. As I'm heading to the car, a woman with a microphone stops me.

"Hi there, I'm with 1010 WINS."

I stare at her blankly. I have no idea what that is. She is kind and patiently explains. "I was hoping to interview you for a few minutes, for our radio show."

"Okay, sure. But only a quick one, we're trying to get to the beach."

Finally, we all headed towards the car. "Quick, let's leave before any other reporters show up."

It's a novel feeling. We all joke about paparazzi. Soon we're on the road, laughing and talking and teasing each other. My phone buzzes.

"Hi, Sarina, it's Melody. Hey, I know you just left, but I wanted to let you know we have another reporter here. From Crain's. He might want to talk with you later. Right now they're taking pictures."

Joking aside, I'm stunned by the attention we're getting. In the end, my conclusion is that all of us, including the journalists, are starved for a good-news story.

Our beach day is fabulous. We grill, we eat and drink, and swim in the ocean. And our customers run our little coffeehouse like pros. Our exercise in love and radical trust has gone wonderfully.

Over the next few days, Melody and I text each other excitedly each time there is a new story about our beach day. All in all, we count over fifteen pieces, and at the end of 2017, our customer takeover is listed in *New York Magazine's* "Reasons to Love New York City."

It's fall, and I remember the kaleidoscope of colors of New England in the autumn. I want to show Elias where I spent my first four years in the US, and show him around the Smith campus and the town of Northampton. We drive under a brilliant blue sky, and I'm struck by how close it is. We're in Northampton in under three hours.

We park the car and walk up Main Street, hand in hand. As we approach the section of Main Street where I remember Haymarket Café, I feel a crushing disappointment. It isn't there. Of course it isn't. It's been over twenty years since I graduated from Smith. But then I see a faded black sign and the narrow entrance, and my heart leaps.

"It's here, Elias! It's here!"

We go in. They've renovated. It looks different, more like a restaurant, but still nice. I scan the room, looking at all the nooks and crannies, checking if there's a corner or a turn or another room I'm missing.

"Elias, oh no . . . the books. The books are gone."

It bothers me that the books are gone. I know even in the early days the books probably didn't make a lot of money. They were used books, as far as I remember. Maybe they had some new ones, but I remember lots and lots of used books. And, of course, books take space. But there's something about the identity and the very being of Haymarket Café that it was a café and also a bookstore. I've moved around so much and have returned over the years to the places I once loved, to fondly remembered old haunts. I am familiar with this bitter-sweetness. I'm so glad that it's still here, but what is here is not the place I remember.

Later I look Haymarket Café up online, to see if I can find out more about what happened. I learn that of the brothers who started the café in 1991, one is no longer an owner. One of them is quoted as saying, "The good books always got stolen, anyway." But Haymarket Café was also in the press in 2016 for signing up for the $15 an hour wage campaign—eliminating tips and paying all their staff $15.50 an hour when minimum wage today in Massachusetts is $11. I learn about their common account, a fund that the community can donate into that allows Haymarket Café to provide a sliding scale menu for people who cannot afford to eat there. Each month there is an update on their website of how many meals are provided through the common account, how much is donated by the community, and what percentage of the retail cost has been covered. And I learned that they are working on bringing more arts, events, and readings to the space, going back to their roots in that way.

Even without the books, the ethos of the original cafe continues. I realize that they continue to draw on the long tradition of coffeehouses. For some reason, I feel deeply relieved by what I've learned.

Before she is famous, before she has ever been covered on the national news, I start following Alexandria Ocasio-Cortez online, and I'm immediately struck by a difference in her message. There is a clarity and courage in her positions that I find profoundly inspiring. Running as a candidate outside the current political system, Alexandria doesn't have anything to lose by being honest and telling it like she sees it. This is so rare in American politics, that it makes me stop, listen, and respond. I start contributing to her primary campaign.

Medicare for All, a living wage, a renewable energy-based economy, these are no-brainers for me. They align with my whole life's work, and are based on a firm belief in international human rights. For so many countries where I have worked, these have been aspirational goals. I let myself imagine what could be possible in the United States, with its immense resources and capabilities, if the political system wasn't hijacked by special interests.

Despite being busy, some would say over-committed, I am intrigued enough to attend one of Alexandria's weekend rallies in the Bronx. My husband and kids drop me off on their way to a play-date with friends. I'm not familiar with the area, and the rally is in a nondescript basement restaurant, but volunteers in the signature "Ocasio2018" purple T-shirts stand outside greeting people. Inside, it is not a large crowd. The group is a small, committed group of volunteers and supporters; there are maybe twenty people in the room. The venue is decorated in baby pink and silver. There is a disco ball hanging from the ceiling and music system is set up. I guess the restaurant must be reserved for a Quinceañera after this event—a fifteenth birthday party important in many Latin cultures. Someone has brought in brownies that look like they're home-baked. A table is stacked with purple T-shirts and campaign buttons—each featuring a policy like Abolish ICE, or Medicare for All. I find out that the buttons have been made by volunteers. On one wall are some maps of the Congressional District, which is a strange one. It incorporates parts of the South Bronx and parts of Queens, and I wondered why it has been drawn up this way.

Alexandria is chatting with some of the guests, animated in her conversation. Her energy is palpable. A few of the super-volunteers from the campaign speak first, talking about the importance of reaching voters, how much they needed people to sign up for phone-banking and door-knocking. Then they hand over to Alexandria. I listen carefully, trying to match what I have observed online to her in-person speech.

She gives a remarkable speech that captures my full attention. She speaks about her own background, about the issues that people in her district are raising. She hardly uses the word "I"; her speech is all about "we." I feel invited to join, invited to be part of a movement. There is no dissonance between what I have read from her Tweets and posts, what was in her campaign video, and what she is saying. She seems genuine, and her message rings true. I have confirmed for myself the excited, inspired feeling I have about her. She impresses the hell out of me—smart, articulate, passionate, and relatable. I think back to 2016, when I wished there had been a candidate that had Bernie Sanders's policy positions and his authenticity, but different demographics. And here she is.

Alexandria's speech doesn't downplay the odds. She is clearly the underdog in primary her race against ten-term incumbent Joe Crowley. But I sense a confidence that there are numbers and a strategy behind this campaign. Alexandria stresses that this last leg of the campaign is the most important. "If you feel tired, keep going, there are more calls to make, there are more doors to knock. This is not the time to be tired, this is the time to push forward." These might not have been her exact words, but I feel her urging us all to push forward, past any barriers, and get this done.

I think it's the alignment between the message and the messenger that I feel most powerfully. I want to help her campaign because I believe in her message, but I also feel strongly that she deeply believes in her message herself.

I sign up without hesitation to be trained to make calls and "phone bank."

"The easiest way to do this is if I can train you all together. Why don't we pick a night when you can all come over to our apartment?" Her name is Simone, and I gather she's an experienced 'super-volunteer' with the campaign. I learn that Simone is also a stand-up comic.

I ask a colleague of mine, someone who I know is impressed with Ocasio-Cortez's candidacy, whether he will join me to be trained and start phone-banking for the campaign. I'm not expecting his enthusiastic yes, but I'm was very glad for it. We go after work on a weeknight, taking the subway to Brooklyn. We take some snacks with us for the group and our hosts.

"You know these people, right?" Jorge asks me.

"Well, I've met them, and I spoke with her for a few minutes." I smile.

We are a little late, but the fact that we have brought snacks seems to make up for it. There are three people in a small living room, and I hear some voices from another room. Two guys are on a computer and phone talking with potential voters, I presume. We are welcomed warmly. As we set up, we see that there is an option for Spanish speakers, and when Jorge suggests that he could make Spanish language calls, his offer is gratefully accepted.

For the first time in my life, I call complete strangers. I ask them if they will consider voting for Alexandria Ocasio-Cortez. Making calls to mostly grumpy strangers is not on my list of favorite things to do, by far, and I get a whole range of responses. Some people hang up. Others sound annoyed. Some engage in conversation. Not many have heard of Ocasio-Cortez. One woman tells me she will vote for Joseph Crowley, Alexandria's opponent, because his wife does good work.

Making these calls in a group helps it be a less isolating experience. If we have a bad call, we can commiserate with each other and trade tips and ideas. The key is to not take the conversations personally. We document the responses on a scale: from supporting her opponent to a strong supporter who can be contacted for volunteer opportunities.

After the dialer closes and we are leaving, I offer to host a phone-banking or postcard writing group at Buunni after hours. I want to do this again, and I know by offering to host at Buunni, I can replicate and expand the efforts of the evening.

A week or so later, I receive 300 postcards and addresses in the mail. I asked Elias to pick up post-card stamps for me from our local post office, but they are sold out. That makes me wonder. This happened right after the Women's March; so many people were writing postcards that it was difficult to find postcard stamps in New York City. But now? I wonder where the demand is coming from, and hope this is a good omen.

Big changes were afoot in Ethiopia after Prime Minister Hailemariam Desalegn stepped down unex-pectedly. His resignation was widely attributed to the prolonged protests led by mainly students and youth over a period of three years. These protests centered in Ethiopia's populous Oromia region, home to almost 35 million Oromos, Ethiopia's largest ethnic group that makes up about 34% of the country's population. While there had been long-standing grievances, this round of protests was sparked in 2015 after a plan was developed to expand the boundaries of the capital, Addis Ababa. The surrounding farmers were worried that the growing city would eat up their lands, and that the government would confiscate their property, leaving them without their way of life, livelihood, or any other options.

The new prime minister, Abiy Ahmed, the forty-one-year-old leader of the Oromo People's Development Organization, was a remarkable choice for many reasons: he was not a career politician, and he spoke movingly about the need for love and understanding, for unity, and for building bridges at a time when many world leaders, including the US president, were talking about building walls and securing borders. Elias and I followed these developments closely. We welcomed this hopeful news, and we also noted the irony in our situation.

The new prime minister made waves in the very first days of taking office. He lifted the state of emergency. The notorious torture jail on the outskirts of Addis Ababa, Ma'ekelawi, was closed. When harrowing reports of torture surfaced in another regional prison, he fired the top five prison officials in the country and admitted the regime had used torture against political opponents. Bloggers and journalists who had been imprisoned were freed, and thousands of political prisoners were pardoned. He then took steps to make peace with neighboring Eritrea, and visited the country and spoke with Eritreans in their own language. About seven months after taking power, Abiy announced his new cabinet, in which half of the ministers are women. Women lead the powerful areas of defense and security, trade, and labor. Each of these actions alone would be deemed newsworthy and important. Taken together, so quickly within the first months of taking power, they were truly historic and momentous.

Abiy's leadership has uplifted Ethiopians at home and abroad. He has encouraged the hundreds of thousands of Ethiopians who make up the diaspora to contribute to the country. Given Ethiopia's severe shortage of foreign currency, a simple and practical way is through the Diaspora Fund, where he is asking Ethiopians working abroad to make a contribution equivalent to a dollar a day. Many who have been in political exile for decades have now traveled back to Ethiopia. When Abiy visited the United States, he met with packed halls of US-based Ethiopians who greeted him like a rock star. Under his leadership, two branches of the Ethiopian Orthodox Church reconciled.

There is talk of "Abiymania," and the term "Ethiopia Dividend" is being used in neighboring countries where some expect his reforms to have a ripple effect. In a world where so much is going wrong, where countries have turned inward, where leaders are talking about building walls, where ships rescuing desperate refugees from the sea are turned away from European ports, and where children are ripped away from their parents' arms at the southern border of the United States, I'll take Abiy Ahmed's call to build bridges and his call for love and inclusivity. It is the music our ears have been straining to hear.

The day comes, and I put on my purple "Ocasio2018" campaign T-shirt. It's the first time I've ever worn a campaign T-shirt, or maybe it's the first time I've ever worn a T-shirt with someone else's name on it. It's normally not my style, but it feels good. I put a poster on our front window and a note that explains what we're doing at Buunni.

I lay out the snacks, turn down the music, and set up the long communal table with postcards, pens, address lists. If I'm honest, I feel a little nervous. Like someone who's hosting a party and is suddenly scared that no guests will show up. I get a text from Jorge that he is running late. Then, a mother and daughter walk in. The mother had called me the day before to confirm, and the daughter has just turned eighteen and will be casting her first-ever vote for Ocasio-Cortez.

Then a couple active in one of the local progressive groups in our neighborhood arrives, and then another couple. I feel relieved. It's going to be okay. I have written a few sample postcards and go over the process with everyone. Soon there is a quiet hum in the room. Eight people in a small neighborhood coffee shop, focused on the task. Handwriting, addressing, placing stamps. Occasionally someone stops and wiggles their fingers, stretches out their palms. Many of us are terribly out of the habit of handwriting anything. Occasionally someone will ask a question or tell an anecdote, but for the most part, we are in focused on our postcards, collegial but quiet.

All three hundred postcards go to voters in Ocasio-Cortez's district ten days before the primary election.

After I get back to New York from my travels, I host a phone-banking party at Buunni. Though calling and talking to strangers is not my favorite way of spending time, I know that it's important, and it's what the campaign needs. And getting a group together makes the task more tolerable—even border-line fun. We're making calls four days before the Primary election. This time I set up the event on the campaign website myself, and I feel more confident in what I'm doing.

Tonight, the conversations feel different. Yes, there are still many hang-ups and people who don't want to talk to us, but many more people have heard of Ocasio-Cortez than the first time I made calls. Many have received a postcard, or someone left materials under their door. Some have already received a call and have decided to vote for her. Others seem more open, and want to know, "Who is she?" The calls in Spanish go particularly well, and I'm so glad to have Jorge making the calls with us. We all cheer after he finishes speaking with a man who promises that he and his whole family will vote for Ocasio-Cortez. The dialer shuts down at 9:00 PM ET by law, and after we all say our good-byes, I text Simone, my contact at the campaign with my update. These calls felt qualitatively different, I think to myself. She's going to do well in this election.

Simone invites me to the primary campaign's official election watch party. I so want to go, but with all my recent travels, I feel guilty about leaving Elias and the kids for another evening. I will spend the evening with my family and watch the results come in online. I snuggle my girls at bed-time, breathing in their sweetness, their soft skin and hair, their insightful right-before-they-fall-asleep questions. Once, Juni took my breath away, sleepy eyed, and almost slurring her words, "Mama, how do you win a war?"

"What do you mean, sweetheart?"

"How do you win a war? What do you have to do to win?"

"Why are you thinking about war right before going to bed? Think about something nice, so you'll have nice dreams." I knew I was dodging the question.

Tonight, the questions aren't so hard. And Juni wishes me luck for "my candidate."

The girls have helped me with the postcards, using yellow highlighters to emphasize certain parts of my message: "Please bring your family and friends to vote on Tuesday, June 26!" or "We have a fantastic candidate!" And I told them both that Alexandria reminded me of them. Strong, smart, honest, and brown. I want them to see examples of young women of color, women who look like them, leading us, particularly in this political environment.

I join Elias in the living room. As is his daily practice, he is watching soccer highlights. I get a tall drink of iced water and sit down with my phone, checking my Twitter feed for the latest. It is still early, and I don't know how much information will be available. But with just a small percentage of the votes in, Ocasio-Cortez looks to be in great shape. I'm now wide awake.

"Elias! Look! Look at this!"

"Oh, wow, she's doing really well."

"Oh. My. God. She can win this thing! She could actually win."

"You did a good job."

"Oh my god. Oh my god. Her numbers just went up! She's leading. She's leading and now more votes are in!"

I get up off the couch and pace around the living room, phone in hand. My heart is beating so fast. I'm so excited, but also so afraid of being crushingly disappointed.

"Elias, her numbers keep going up."

My husband, the math wizard, is counting her lead and looking at the percentage of the votes that are in.

"It looks like she's going to win."

"Oh my god, Elias. Are you sure? They're going to call it for her soon. Put the TV on, now she might finally be on TV!"

The first channel we put on is CNN, not expecting to see anything, but there it is, Ocasio-Cortez with 57.6% of the vote, the projected winner. I'm hugging my husband and hyperventilating. A part of me is kicking myself for not being at the watch party to take in the mood, to take in what is surely a historic moment. The other part of me, totally content in this moment, home with my family, so proud of the tiny part I have played. As soon as I can stop hugging Elias, I text Jorge.

Are you watching the results???

YES!!!!! YES!!!!!!

OMG!!!!

This is happening.

This is amazing. Yes!!

I text my congratulations to Simone. I pace around some more. Wow. It feels amazing to win.

I arrive in London at Gatwick Airport for a WaterAid meeting. There is a huge line at the passport control. There are signs that say UK border. I observe myself, passport and form in hand in the non-EU line, tired from the overnight red-eye flight from New York. A woman is walking past us, urgently, and then circles around again, looking into the crowd. The woman ahead of me steps aside to give her way, and the woman says, "My daughter, I'm looking for my daughter."

I can see her worry escalating into a panic. She is weaving through the long line, looking here and there. Those around her are looking around to see if we can spot a lost child. The chattering crowd is suddenly quiet. All of us are caught up in the moment, and in this mother's contagious fear.

Behind us we hear a voice, "Mama!"

The woman's whole body changes, like she is letting go of a thousand breaths she has been holding in. As I exhale, I realize I've been holding my breath too. She rushes to her daughter, hugs her, and tightly holds onto her hand as they start walking. I would guess that her daughter is about nine years old.

I think of another border. Other mothers and fathers. The panic and the grief of the families who have been separated at the southern border of the United States. When I think of them, when I think of the young children separated from their families, I have to stop and catch my breath. If I can't bear to think about it too deeply, how are they living through it? The pain, the trauma, and the suffering that this administration has unleashed is so unnecessary, and now I'm weeping at Gatwick Airport because this small moment has brought home with a gut punch the reality of what our government is doing to some of the most vulnerable people in the world.

Before I left on my trip, I taught my two daughters my and my husband's phone numbers. I repeated the numbers with them, making sing-song verses out of the ten digits, and I tested them until they could confidently recite each. I first taught them my number, then, realizing I would be away, I taught them their dad's. It's the first time I've made them memorize anything, but I had read recently about a six-year-old girl who was reunited with her family because she happened to know their phone numbers. It suddenly seemed imperative.

One evening at home, Juni must have overheard parts of my conversation with Elias. She said to me, "Mama, I don't ever want to leave the country, because when we come back from our trip, what if they take us away from you?"

"Juni, baby, when we go on trips we come back through the airport. That's not the border we're talking about. No one's going to take you away from me."

My words had a hollow ring. There's a task force to "de-naturalize" naturalized citizens. Was I telling my daughter the truth? Do I believe this myself? I don't know. I just don't know.

Juni is now eight years old and she cries when I'm leaving on a trip, though she knows I'll be back. She wants to cuddle in bed with me, and she tells me the most important things that are on her mind in those quiet moments in the dark, just before she falls asleep. Maya is four. I've tried to count how many times in a day she might say "Mama!" in her insistent tone, wanting to show me something, wanting me to admire her antics, kiss her elbow better, find her hair band, tell me a joke, or tell me she loves me. Every time I try to count, I get distracted and lose count around twenty-something. These days, as we go through our daily routines, I can't stop thinking about the children who have been detained and separated—no, kidnapped, stolen away—from their parents as they arrived at the US after a long and arduous journey seeking refuge, or simply a better life. Those children need their mamis and papis. Some of them are crying out.

Others have stopped crying. Dogged local journalism has revealed terrible conditions, freezing rooms, children forbidden to comfort or console each other, and now we are learning of children seven and eight years old who have died in custody of the US government. In the pit of my stomach, I know we don't yet know the worst of it yet. Organizations and immigration attorneys have stepped up their efforts and are sharing the stories that their clients are telling them. But one day, we will know a lot more, and a lot worse.

I haven't said this to anyone yet, but lately I've been wondering about a back-up plan. If things get worse in this country, don't I owe it to my kids to get us out of here? When is it bad enough to leave? Should we leave because we are complicit? My taxes and yours are paying for the injustices that America is sowing. For mass incarceration, for private prisons, for the deaths of innocents in countless countries. Our taxes are used to pay for needless suffering. Our taxes wreak havoc on the lives of some of the most vulnerable people on the planet, both here at home and overseas.

Do we close up and leave? Start again some-where else? We are in the middle of growing our business and raising our family. We've invested our labor and our love in this country. We've given up a lot to come to this country, and have a lot to con-tribute to it. We came because we believed in the idea of America, and its promise. Is it not our job to make it live up to its ideals? After all this, are we supposed to give up without a fight? Isn't this coun-try, as flawed as it is, worth fighting for? Maybe it's us, the immigrants and the refugees who have fallen hard for the American dream, that must fight hard-est to make it come true.

Or is it time to wake up and realize that the dream we thought we were chasing is a terrible nightmare in the cold light of day? The racism, the white supremacy, the gun violence, the war econ-omy, the individualism taken to extremes that leaves little room for empathy or compassion—when I think about these things, I think I should get my kids the hell out of here. Our decision, to stay or to go, will shape their whole lives.

The world is big and beautiful and messy. And there is so much more to the world than America. I don't want my children to be constrained by the way they are seen here. I want them to be proud and unafraid, and never feel that they are less than anyone else. I hate the uncertainty that shows up in small, everyday decisions. We're planning a summer vacation and we'd love to explore this gorgeous country, visit parts that we haven't been to yet. But I hesitate, I worry about our physical safety, but even more insidiously I worry if our family, brown and bronze-hued, will be made to feel unwelcome. The whole point of a vacation is to relax. Maybe we should stick to the high-melanin parts of the country.

I want my children to be free to explore and roam their country. We imagined a life expansive and unafraid, but today we are starting to feel confined.

I want another win. Partly instinct and partly the result of my research and recent political education, I feel there is a real opportunity at the local and state level. My first step is to connect with local "challenger" campaigns in New York. With a population of almost twenty million people, the fourth most populous state in the country, a change in New York would be significant. A state that one would think would be leading the charge, that would be a secure and true sanctuary for immigrants. A state that should be leading the country in progressive legislation.

The reality, as I've been learning these past two years, is quite the opposite. Our state politics are in a sad state: New York makes it extremely difficult for people to vote, and therefore has one of the lowest voter turnout rates in the country.

Right after the 2016 election, I remember counting New York's immigrant-friendly identity as a blessing, but I've come to realize that there is very little actual legal protection for immigrants. For almost two years now, Amanda, a Guatemalan woman, has sought refuge in a church in our neighborhood because she is afraid ICE will deport her away from her three children.

Buunni is now supporting and connected to local campaigns, and I feel energized and inspired by these small actions. It's a welcome change from feeling depressed or hand-wringing and head-shaking. I feel fueled by these actions. I'm still angry and heartbroken about what's happening in our country. But through the small actions I'm taking, I'm finding a world of hope and possibility.

White supremacists gathered today in Fort Tryon Park, the gem of our neighborhood. I wouldn't have believed it until it happened. That it could happen in a neighborhood in New York City is shocking to me; that it could happen in our neighborhood is deeply disquieting. This is where we go sledding in the winter and picnic in the summer. Our brown children have frolicked in delight and rolled around in their tantrums here. Our park has been defiled.

The group, which was part of the white supremacist rally in Charlottesville, photographed themselves (no face shots) and published the images widely on social media. They were making a statement.

I had not heard of the group before looking them up online. The Southern Poverty Law Center had an extensive write-up on them, and designates them as a hate group. In the last two years, their membership has grown from two digits to over a thousand people. By the end of 2018, they plan to reach 5,000 members. The leaders o the group itself credit the "Trump effect" for the massive growth in their membership. After the "Unite the Right" rally in Charlottesville that ended with many injured and the death of Heather Heyer, the group rebranded themselves a more moderate white "iden-titarian" movement.

In addition to the photos distributed by the group itself, a video emerges taken by someone at the park. I marvel at the man's bravery, the wobbly phone video showing him being taunted and threatened. He stands his ground and continues videoing. The people being recorded didn't seem worried about their full faces being on view. They are done hiding their beliefs, and in line with their strategy of "claiming spaces," they are trying to claim our beloved Fort Tryon Park. This is in a part of Manhattan where Spanish is at least as widely spoken as, if not more commonly spoken than, English.

The next evening, many members of our community, including elected officials, gather at the park in solidarity, and to express their rejection of hate—to claim and reclaim our neighborhood. When people say that this administration, this president, has emboldened the racists, I knew there were lots of examples. This one, however, hits home.

There's a flurry of activities in the weeks that follow. Campaigns are gearing up, candidates are endorsing each other, and there seem to be so many candidates that it's hard to keep track. The energy that's building is palpable. There is a huge range, a spectrum, of candidates all along the Democratic Party platform. Those that I'm most excited about are those who don't have a lot to lose. They are fresh, they have something to say, and they are not scared to say it. They are the underdogs, the unlikely candidates, and supporting them is an act of faith. But as their momentum and their numbers grow, politics is becoming exciting. Not having many allies within "establishment" politics, these candidates are endorsing each other, creating moments and photo-opportunities for themselves. They are supporting and lifting each other up, and this is particularly visible among the female candidates, of which there are record numbers at every level.

One evening, we are writing postcards as a family activity, the kids coloring and drawing on them, arguing over who gets to stick the "sticker stamps."

Juni says, "Mama, this is such a win-win."

I smile at her use of the phrase. It's the first time I've heard her use it.

"Because," she continues, "there are other people at home, too, in families, and you can get them to vote by mail, too, so you get more votes for your voter [she means candidate] by doing voting by mail."

What can I say? My kid has got smarts.

After a summer of massive organizing, phone banking, texting, postcard writing, and most importantly, canvassing and door knocking, the New York State primary elections take place. The state senate races have become surprisingly competitive; each of the former "IDC" members (who ran as Democrats but caucused with Republicans, preventing a Democratic majority) have challengers running against them. As it turns out, our two coffee shops are in districts that have IDC members up for reelection. In Riverdale, Alessandra Biaggi is running to challenge the leader and main deal-maker behind the IDC.

After the kids go to bed, I go to our friends Dana and Robert, who conveniently, are also our next-door neighbors, and a core part of our adopted extended family in New York. If our girls could, they would drill a door through the wall that separates our apartments. Dana, Robert, and I sit in their comfortable living room, watching the results start to come in. I'm sitting on the edge of their dark blue couch, full of adrenaline and hope.

Challengers in the state-wide roles of governor, lieutenant governor, and attorney general all lose to their more mainstream, politically experienced and generously financed opponents. As disappointing as this is, the real news of the night is about the New York State Senate. As these results start to come in, I can barely sit still. Some of the candidates I'm rooting for lose, but six out of the seven members of the IDC, including its leader, are defeated. The two IDC challengers that we had supported through Buunni both win their races. In all, it is a political earthquake in New York—and in New York City. In one swoop, these candidates make the New York State Senate younger, more female, and more inclusive of people of color. They have also exposed and ousted a bizarre and corrupt political deal that had continued for years under the radar.

After Alexandria Ocasio-Cortez, this is the next big political upset in New York, and it has been hard won, once again fueled by the work of volunteers, smart digital strategy, and most of all, by face-to-face voter contact—by talking to people, looking them in the eye (no easy feat in New York City), and getting them excited about a political change.

There are so many things I love about New York, but the lifestyle still sometimes feels unnatural. How can it be that I see my children for about an hour and half in the morning and a similar hour and a half in the evening on weekdays? As they grow into fascinating, individual beings, there are so many things about them that are mysteries. I make up for the lost time by holding them close to me evenings and mornings, and weekends, but most of our weekday hours are spent away from each other.

Then there are the luxuries like this one. We're traveling to Dallas, for a family wedding; my mom, Juni, and I have a hotel room together, and the type of time that is increasingly precious to me. Physically close during the day, and at night Juni and I sleep in the same bed. These three days there are no big arguments. We are both relaxed. I'm present, having decided to unplug from work. Sometimes Juni swims and I read, or she reads and I talk to my mom, or Juni is dancing at the wedding and I'm chatting with relatives at a table nearby. We're together, and that is relaxing, even when we aren't directly interacting with each other. She knows I'm near and not going anywhere, and so she doesn't cling, or ask for endless stories or games or

activities. We just are. Sometimes we talk and sometimes we don't, and it's all okay. That's the type of
time I crave with my children.

I try to build these moments into a daily routine, but it's hard. I'm either immersed in home life
or I'm immersed in work life, and one doesn't leave
room for the other. When I go to work in the morning, I am whole, multi-faceted, thinking about home
things and work things. But when I get to the office,
within forty-five minutes I am in a work tunnel. It
can be exciting or exhausting, but there isn't much
else. It's a rare day that I call my husband in the
middle of the day. One time he had dental surgery
and I forgot to call him from work to check in on
him. I was so ashamed.

I normally emerge from my "work tunnel" at
about 5PM. And then I'll remember that I've forgotten some very important things. There is either this
or that, but not both at the same time. Sometimes
I feel embarrassed about it. Then I try to justify it.
When I'm with my family, I tell myself, I'm not
thinking about work either.

There are so many blessings, big and small. This
weekend I'm trying to teach the girls how to make
their beds.

"Juni, you know taking care of your things, your
surroundings, is part of taking care of yourself. It's
really important in life to be organized."

"Yes, but Mama, it's also really important in life to like reading and math and science."

I smile. She's highlighting her strengths and isn't saying anything I could disagree with.

I am struck by the air and the excitement, like a large sporting event. Anticipation, predictions, and I'm pretty sure bets are being made. Like a horse-race. This one is leading . . . now that one . . . now the other can't possibly make a comeback! There's an eagerness to predict the outcome, to call the result, to be the first to do so. Have I just not noticed this before? It would all be very entertaining, but it's not a sports event, it's the midterm elections.

So many things are broken—literally broken. In New York, there are widespread reports of broken machines, including some locations where every single ballot machine is broken. Some voters have the luxury of staying in line and waiting, but for most others, regardless of what the law says, their employers won't take kindly to their missing a shift without prior notice. Even if someone budgets ample time, who plans on waiting three hours at the polling station?

In the end, many future-predictors and data wizards are taken aback by the midterm results—many of which are historic firsts. I am heartened to see more brown and black women in office. Some were running as the underdog and have been outspent by orders of magnitude. The melanin content of the House of Representatives has gone up, the average age has gone down, and in 2019, the percentage of women in Congress will finally exceed 20%. It will stand at the highest ever: 23.4%. This is still so far from any kind of parity, but I don't want to discount this step towards a more representative democracy. At the same time, the fact that the broadening representation is happening entirely in one of the two political parties doesn't feel like a good sign of health for American democracy.

It's not just that women got elected. For me, the most exciting part of the election results are the types of women who were elected. While they may represent many "firsts"—the youngest, the first two Muslims, the first two Native Americans, the first African American from her city, or state—they have come to Congress having done their homework. They have strong policy positions and legislative priorities. They are clear-voiced and unapologetic. They are lifting up each other's voices and supporting each other. The newest members of Congress are a breath of fresh air in an institution that has a dismal recent record, and they are an affirmation of the sense of possibility that I hold dear about this country. From Minnesota, Ilhan Omar, a hijabi Muslim and former refugee, is now a US member of Congress governing our country. Alexandria Ocasio-Cortez pulled off a huge upset and brings her lived working-class experience unapologetically to Congress. They are smart, they are articulate, and they are inspiring.

If I am truly honest, a part of me is so unused to putting my trust in politicians that I am already preparing myself for what I tell myself will be inevitable disappointments. And, I am ready to hold them to account, to live up to their promises and the immense sense of hope and possibility they embody for so many of us who have never seen ourselves in those who govern this country. Another truth: for me, moving from being a bystander to finally finding my own political voice has been exhilarating.

Chaos and cruelty continue as the preferred policy of the administration—the latest atrocities include tear gas being used against families and children at the Southern border, and two children, aged seven and eight, who have died in US government custody. We don't even yet know the worst of it, I think whenever I see another horrific story reported.

At the same time, the space on the other side seems to be widening. Policies that only recently were considered so radical that they wouldn't get a public airing are now being discussed and debated in the mainstream. Youth mobilizing and organizing for a Green New Deal, the movement against gun violence, the movement for healthcare as a human right, and for Medicare for All—the early seeds of a public imagining of what could be possible if America were not entangled in endless war.

To paraphrase Ilhan Omar, our new representatives have not come to play.

Elias and I have just celebrated our ninth wedding anniversary and our fourteenth year of being together. Appropriately, we are in our car, he is driving, and I'm talking with him, whizzing through our joint to-do list: email the architect, respond to the baker, call Con Edison, book the babysitter, e-mail my board chair. I am working both of our phones simultaneously. There is a lull between finishing this group of tasks and starting the next; our work together never ends, but there are lulls, and here is one.

"Elias, man, it's our wedding anniversary. We should talk about the last nine years. What was the big thing in each year?" I like these conversations.

"2009, we got married," he starts. I can hear the smile in his voice.

"2010, Juneli was born."

"2011, well, we moved to New York!"

"2012, we started Buunni."

"2013, Maya was born."

"2014, I started my job as CEO of WaterAid."

"2015 . . . maybe in 2015 we just survived and recovered from all this. Actually, no! We signed the lease for expanding Buunni into the Bus Terminal." By this time, we're both smiling from ear to ear.

"Okay, okay, let's keep going."

"2016, no idea where 2016 went."

"2017, we started Buunni in Riverdale."

"And there you go, here we are in 2018. Elias, are we completely nuts?"

"Well, we were together five years before we got married. Those years we relaxed. We got to know each other properly, we traveled, we enjoyed."

"Thank goodness for that. Now we're definitely not relaxed, but we're still having fun."

As I'm writing this, we are still waiting to complete our long-awaited space at the George Washington Bridge Bus Terminal in Washington Heights. Buunni in Riverdale in the Bronx finally opened about six months ago. And we are still in discussions with another independent coffeehouse about taking over their business, so they can exit and pursue their other dreams. Elias eventually wants to start roasting coffee again. I want to continue to nurture community conversations, organizing, and action. I want to reclaim the rich legacy of coffeehouse politics and apply it to our time. The process of growing Buunni as a business could be a whole other book. We tell each other that we are planting the seeds right now, and we hope our harvest is good. Like growing great coffee, this requires carefully balancing tremendous risk and opportunity.

But in this political and economic climate, our story is becoming less likely. By vilifying immigrants, this administration is nurturing the deep roots of racism in America. At the same time, small businesses like ours face an existential threat in New York City, the sky-rocketing rents are partly due to the nefarious dealings between politicians, landlords, and the real-estate industry. At the same time, small businesses are being squeezed out by the influence and power concentrated in a few corporations voraciously taking over and replacing retail and community-facing businesses. The growing numbers of empty and shuttered storefronts in Manhattan are visible markers that something is deeply wrong. We worry about both these trends and how they will impact our immediate family, and also our broader kinship of immigrants and small businesses. Yet, we continue to invest our labor, our love, and our hope in this country. It is our home, and we are determined to do the work to make it live up to its potential.

A string of lights entwines the microphone. The keyboard and amps are set against the window, which looks different, festive and intimate at the same time. The lights are low, there's wine, cheese, and crackers, and as people start to crowd in, I notice a woman rocking on the balls of her feet, generating an energy; she's quietly preparing, practicing. We're hosting a variety show at Buunni. Our neighborhood is brimming with creative talent—musicians, actors, artists, professional and amateur—and we've had a good response. One of our baristas is a singer and musician and has taken charge of putting these shows together. As the performance begins, there's a powerful feeling of togetherness and support. I'm moved by the sheer talent, as well as the bravery of the new performers. After one woman finishes her song, she tells us it's the first time she's ever sung for an audience. We cheer and clap loudly and we mean it.

In a tiny space, a dancer performs and my heart leaps with her moves. The energy, beauty, and grace of her movements somehow expand the space we're in. She could be up on the biggest stage. We laugh as a storyteller regales us with her tale of utter humiliation, and we cringe with her, feeling every emotion she describes. A well-known performer plays piano and sings—his eclectic choice of songs, some funny, some painful and raw, brings more emotion to the room. A young man, who I'm told plays on Broadway, and his friend do a jazz piece that has the whole room nodding and swaying. A Buunni regular who often writes in his journal in the café confided to me a few days before about his nervousness in performing. But he's there with his guitar and the songs that he has written, and they are beautiful, specific in Uptown references, but also universal songs of love and loss.

I'm enthralled. I look around me and people are smiling, swaying, nodding in encouragement. I don't want to forget this moment. I want to remember every detail, but most of all, I want to remember what this moment of connection feels like. How something so simple can be so powerful. There is a beauty in the room, in this small, crowded, cramped space. I'm reminded that art is essential, therapeutic, and healing. My heart is suddenly full, and I feel an aching hope. There's so much passion and pain in this room, but most importantly, there is love, and that's what makes it home.

POST NOTE

THERE'S UNDOUBTEDLY a community-connection-fueled power at the small, independent, local coffeehouse. I think again of the over eight hundred of us coffeehouses that responded so quickly and contributed to the ACLU fundraiser all around the country. What a difference we can make, understanding our neighborhoods as we do, and having a real relationship with people in our communities. What could we accomplish if we could make the coffeehouse politically relevant again? Not partisan, but politically engaged and active. If we can reject this newfound notion of a sterile, neutral environment of isolated individual coffee consumption, and instead embrace a more raucous and messier but ultimately much more fulfilling space for debate and dialogue.

I'm in. Those of you who are in the coffee community, I invite you to join in the coffeehouse resistance. Those who have already taken the leap, let's share our stories widely. Tag #CoffeehouseResistance so that we can all follow along. Those of you who go to coffeehouses, I invite you to start a conversation with someone you don't know. Those of you who are starting to feel excited, seek out your local coffeehouse owners and talk to them about reclaiming their historical legacy as a place for conversation and political action. Invite me to your own local coffeehouse, where I would love to continue these conversations.

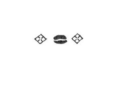

ACKNOWLEDGMENTS

I owe a lifetime of thanks. So many people have supported me, believed in me, and taught me. I have not named them all, but I cherish them all.

My parents, Satish and Sheila, are the solid ground I've always returned to—each nourishing different but essential parts of my being. My love and life (and now business) partner, Elias, clears my path and he's done it again. My daughters keep me honest—and keep me laughing and learning every day.

This book was written a few pages at a time: a jet-lagged morning in a hotel room, a dehydrated hour during a transatlantic flight, the all-too-short quiet of writing night at Buunni, the camaraderie of the Gotham Writers memoir class taught by Carmen Bugan, occasionally at home amidst two girls giggling, screaming, and sometimes climbing all over me. The first time I wrote for hours, undisturbed, was at the magical When Words Count Retreat nestled among the Green Mountains of Vermont. I'd like to thank Steve Eisner for welcoming me—and my whole family—at the retreat; and Amber Griffith for her art form, delicious, thoughtfully prepared meals, of which she is a master.

My publisher, Dede Cummings, of Green Writers Press is enthusiastically supportive, my editor, Rose Alexandre-Leach, has improved this book immeasurably, and my publicist, Ben Tanzer, is also an excellent brainstorming partner.. Friends and colleagues have read and provided feedback on the manuscript in part or in whole: I'd like to thank Marilyn Atlas, Carmen Bugan, Athos Cakiades, Sara Kelleher, Sue Lisk, Melody Morrow, Celine Schmidt, Jennifer Young, Peggy Moran, and Aurvi Sharma.

ABOUT THE AUTHOR

SARINA PRABASI has lived the life of a global nomad and is a new American. She was born in the Netherlands to Nepali parents and was raised in India, China, and Nepal, after which she spent formative years in the United States and in Ethiopia. Sarina is a seasoned leader in international development—working on global health, education, water, and sanitation for over 25 years. In 2011, she moved from Addis Ababa to New York City and started Buunni Coffee with her husband. Their small business has become a hub for community conversation and action. Sarina is the proud mama of two daughters, who keep her learning and laughing every day.

A NOTE ON THE TYPE

The Coffeehouse Resistance: Brewing Hope in Desperate Times was typset in Dante, a mid-20th-century book typeface designed by Giovanni Mardersteig, originally for use by the Officina Bodoni. The original type was cut by Charles Malin. The type is a serif face influenced by (but not directly indebted to) the types cut by Francesco Griffo between 1449 and 1516. Mardersteig had become acquainted with Griffo's type in the design of his previous typeface, called Griffo. One of the primary objectives in designing Dante was in keeping a visual balance between the roman and italics (in Griffo's time typefaces were cut in roman style and italic style, but not both).

The name of the typeface comes from the first book in which it was first used, Boccaccio's Trattatello in Laude di Dante, published in 1955 by the Officina Bodoni. The book used types cut by Malin between 1946 and 1952. The date of the typeface is sometimes given as 1954. Dante would become one of the most used types by Mardersteig.

Originally Dante was cut for use on the private handpress, but Monotype had already expressed interest in issuing Dante for machine composition before 1955. This was about the same time that Malin died, and Monotype was also interested in adding a semibold weight to the Dante family. Matthew Carter, in his twenties at the time, was recruited to cut some of the initial punches of the semibold. Monotype issued its Dante in 1957. Dante was redrawn for digital use by Monotype's Ron Carpenter in 1993.

DESIGNED BY DEDE CUMMINGS

ORNAMENT / DINGBAT CREATED BY ELIZABETH LEIH